MODELS OF THE KINGDOM

Models
of the
Kingdom

Some say God rules the heart.
Some say the church.
Some say the cosmos.
Some say human history.
Some say they need no king.

HOWARD A. SNYDER

ABINGDON PRESS / Nashville

MODELS OF THE KINGDOM

Copyright © 1991 by Abingdon Press

This book is printed on recycled, acid-free paper.

Library of Congress Cataloging-in-Publication Data

Snyder, Howard A
    Models of the kingdom / Howard A. Snyder.
      p. cm.
    Includes index.
    ISBN 0-687-27104-5
    1. Kingdom of God.   2. Typology (Theology)   I. Title.
    BT94.S647   1991   91-17858
    231.7'2—dc20   CIP

Scripture quotations, unless otherwise indicated, are from the *Holy Bible: New International Version*. Copyright © 1973, 1978, 1984 by the International Bible Society. Used by permission of Zondervan Bible Publishers.

Those noted NRSV are from the New Revised Standard Version Bible, copyright © 1989 by the Division of Christian Education of the National Council of the Churches of Christ in the United States of America.

Those noted KJV are from the King James Version of the Bible.

Excerpts from "An Earthly Theological Agenda," by Sallie McFague, copyright 1991 Christian Century Foundation. Reprinted by permission from the January 2-9, 1991 issue of *The Christian Century*.

Excerpts from *The Word of Life* (Volume II of SYSTEMATIC THEORY) by Thomas C. Oden. Reprinted by permission of Harper Collins Publishers.

MANUFACTURED IN THE UNITED STATES OF AMERICA

In memory of
Mark Mason,
friend and brother,
who struggled with the meaning of God's kingdom

PREFACE

MENTION THE term "kingdom of God" and you quickly discover that the church is divided into different camps. One thinks the kingdom is the hottest topic around; another thinks that talking about the kingdom is like digging up fossils. Other people seem puzzled that anyone would even raise the issue.

The interesting thing is that these camps are hardly aware of each other. Yet together they illustrate one of the thrusts of this book: What we think about the kingdom of God is a clue to our understanding of the gospel itself.

This book explores the meaning of the gospel through the lens of varying understandings of God's reign. It employs an eightfold typology that I have developed and tested over the past several years.

The book owes much to many people, both directly and indirectly. The community of students and faculty at United Theological Seminary has stimulated and sharpened my thinking on a number of issues dealt with in the book. I am especially grateful to faculty colleagues Donald Gorrell, James Nelson, and Tyron Inbody for critiquing an early draft of my typology and offering helpful suggestions. My editor at Abingdon Press, Paul Franklyn, displayed a careful sensitivity to my intended meaning. The book is better for it, and I am glad to acknowledge this help as well.

C O N T E N T S

INTRODUCTION

THIS BOOK examines different conceptions of the kingdom of God by outlining eight "models" or basic metaphors for understanding God's reign. While the focus is the "kingdom" or reign of God, the basic issue is how God's saving work in the world may be understood and experienced.

We all have models in our heads—models of what God is like, what church and family should be, and where history is going. This book is about models of the kingdom: the ways we perceive God's activity in the world and in our lives.

For some people, God is a King with a heavenly army; for others, an Architect with a plan; for still others, the Parent of a worldwide family. All these models say something about what theology has traditionally called the kingdom of God.

Imagine a church meeting in which half a dozen leaders are deciding whether the church should open its doors to feed homeless people. We hear several responses:

"We *should* be doing this. Jesus came to minister to the poor and needy."

"But is this going to meet their spiritual needs?"

"Should we have a worship service in connection with the meals?"

"What we really should do is work for more job opportunities in this city."

"Do you realize the problems this could mean for keeping the church clean?"

"I think feeding the hungry is really what the gospel is all about."

Here we have differing perspectives and, very likely, different models of the kingdom. For some, the work of the kingdom is spiritual; for others, it is material. To some people, kingdom work is church work; to others, it is changing social structures. As this example illustrates, models are not just opinions or theories; they are often the lenses through which we view reality.

Models of the kingdom of God can have earth-shaking results, as we will see in this book. What people believe about the kingdom often shapes what they do. As Jerald C. Brauer wrote, "The kingdom of God is one of the most fruitful yet controversial concepts in Christian theology. It has been employed to uphold the status quo, and it has been a revolutionary ideal used to break social forms and customs."[1] Controversy still surrounds the concept; today some attack the very idea of "kingdom" as anachronistic, irrelevant, or even oppressive.

It is no secret that there has been a new surge of interest in the kingdom of God in recent decades. What may surprise some is the extent, the *breadth* of this interest. Fresh discussions and explorations of the kingdom theme have emerged around the globe in a wide variety of Christian traditions, and at popular, as well as scholarly, levels of the church. Dozens of books were published in English on this topic during the 1980s. It has been a major theme of the World Council of Churches and of various conferences or symposia in a variety of traditions. An ongoing dialogue between charismatic Christians and evangelical social activists brought together some forty Christians from fifteen nations for several days of discussion near London, England, around the theme "The Spirit and the Kingdom" in January 1990. And one of the fastest growing contemporary Christian movements, Vineyard Christian Fellowship, takes the kingdom of God as the starting point of its theology.

No doubt there are many reasons for new interest in the kingdom today, and we will want to explore some of these. Underlying all others, however, are two in particular: the shrinking of the globe into one earth society, and what I have elsewhere called the new internationalization of the church.[2] These two megatrends, I believe, are altering the consciousness of people generally and of Christians in particular throughout the earth. Author Garry Wills points to another possible factor: the decade of the nineties. "The ending of a century in the year 2000 . . . is bound to create that feeling of history taking a corner that always stimulates apocalyptic thinking," he writes. "An understanding of Christian prophecy will be more needed, not less, in the next few years, as 'signs of the times' are read by everyone under the impending deadline of a millennium."[3]

The Christian church has always believed it had a world gospel and (generally) that it had a message of salvation to be proclaimed "to the ends of the earth" (Acts 1:8). But now the ends of the earth have met each other. We travel around the globe and daily we hear news from every "corner" of the earth. More to the point: Christians are found now in virtually every nation and in an increasing number of earth's estimated 60,000 people groups. And something new is beginning to happen: Wherever they exist on earth, believers are coming to see themselves as part of one worldwide church in an increasingly interconnected world.

Heightened interest in the kingdom of God does not, however, necessarily mean a clearer understanding of what God's kingdom *is*. People from varying backgrounds may hold quite different conceptions of the kingdom, even when they claim to take Scripture as their starting point. So a renewed interest in God's reign may lead to confusion even as it provokes useful discussion. My hope is to clarify the discussion by sorting through differing conceptions of the kingdom.

My own interest in the kingdom has grown directly out of my concern with church renewal. The disturbing split between what the church often *is* as we see it and what it is *called to be* in Scripture led me to examine not only the structure but also the mission of the church. This in turn led to a consideration of God's overall "plan"—the "mission of God," as some put it—which in turn led directly to the question of the kingdom. It became clear to me in examining the Scriptures that one can't speak of the mission of the church without dealing with the kingdom. This is most striking in the Gospel records about Jesus himself, the one who came announcing that the kingdom of God had drawn near.

I explored in a preliminary way this broader perspective for looking at the church in *The Community of the King*. Later in *A Kingdom Manifesto,* I attempted to outline a biblical theology of the kingdom, showing how such a perspective affects our understanding and practice of church.[4] The more I dealt with this theme, however, the more I saw that people could mean very different and even contrary things by "kingdom of God." Hence the need for this book. My hope is that sorting out several clearly different conceptions of God's reign will lead to greater clarity about this key theme and ultimately to a more faithful obedience to Jesus' words about seeking first God's kingdom (Matt. 6:33). More personally, this book represents a sort of testimony and report on my own spiritual and theological explorations back and forth across the spectrum treated here.

Much of the Christian conception of the kingdom derives from Jesus' teachings as reported in the Gospels. This raises the question of whether the Gospels give us Jesus' own words, those of the Gospel writers, or later views of the church. My own opinion is that the Gospels give us substantially the words of Jesus, though often summarized or paraphrased. Generally I will attribute sayings to Jesus that in the Gospels are attributed to him without adding "according to Matthew" or "according to Luke." The references will make clear what the written source is, and readers who are less confident about the original source of the words can make their own allowances. This matter has some significance for our discussion of varying models, of course—whether we are dealing with a certain ambiguity and "mystery" in Jesus' own teachings or whether apparent differences in viewpoint represent later Christian "traditions in conflict."[5] I will argue that several key tensions or polarities in understanding the kingdom are found in Jesus' own teachings as well as in other biblical writings. In any case, clearly the Scriptures do give us a range of teachings and sayings about the kingdom.

The plan of the book is as follows: Chapter 1 shows the usefulness of "models" in considering the kingdom of God and introduces eight basic models. Chapters 2 through 9 then delineate these models. In each case the method will be to briefly describe the model, discuss its biblical basis, and present several examples. Some strengths and limitations of each model will also be noted. Then chapter 10 compares the models, dealing with the question of how we may discern an understanding of God's reign today that is biblically faithful, theologically sound, and relevant in our present age.

The last two chapters draw out some practical meanings of God's reign, looking first globally and then locally. Our final destination will be several suggestions for embodying the truth of God's kingdom in local congregations that want to "seek first [God's] kingdom and his righteousness" (Matt. 6:33).

I have attempted throughout the book to provide striking examples from across the nearly two thousand years of church history. One of the values of ranging across the historical spectrum is that one sees how similar themes keep recurring. Doctrines and emphases that appear at various times in history are not totally unique to the particular period or people who espouse them. Such a historical overview does, of course, run the risk of oversimplification or of forcing rather complex ideas into an artificial framework. On the other hand, it can be immensely helpful for people to learn that things they have been taught (and that perhaps have been seen as distinctive or unique to their tradition) have in fact been taught and believed in other times and places—and perhaps as part of a quite different set of assumptions. This may indeed be the case here as we examine various kingdom models and illustrate them from history.

1 THE MYSTERY OF THE KINGDOM AND THE USE OF MODELS

U SING MODELS in dealing with the kingdom of God is a way of seeking to dispel the vague cloud of confusion that often forms around this theme. Rather than a primarily biblical exposition of the kingdom, my approach here is essentially theological and historical. The methodology is similar to that of Avery Dulles in his books *Models of the Church* and *Models of Revelation.*[1] Like Dulles and a number of other authors, I find models a useful methodology for clarifying theological issues.[2]

Since the kingdom theme raises the question of the church's role in society, this book also addresses some of the issues discussed in H. Richard Niebuhr's *Christ and Culture.*[3]

Dulles observes, "Typological thinking is characteristic of periods when cultural and ideological pluralism abounds. It tends to go with a somewhat skeptical and critical mentality—one that sees the limitations of every theory and commitment."[4] We now live in such a time. Thinking people are keenly aware of beliefs and world views other than their own. For the Christian, this raises questions: How broadly is what I believe about my faith really true? Is it true for me only, or only for the church or those who consider themselves Christians? Or is Christian teaching true for all times, places, and peoples? If so, in what sense, since the church has not always taught precisely the same thing?

The use of types and models may be a way of dodging such questions or a way of facing them head-on. Models are appealing in part because they presuppose diversity in belief. My approach here is not to skirt the issue of truth, however, nor simply to describe some possible options for discussion or intellectual assent. It is, rather, to use models as a way of getting at the truth of the kingdom. Thus we will not only describe models and raise the question of their evaluation, but we will also consider the question of discerning those understandings of the kingdom that are most consistent with the character of Jesus Christ. Ultimately for the Christian a valid conception of the kingdom (in theory and practice) must meet three tests: It must (1) be solidly grounded in Scripture, (2) be true to the character of Jesus Christ as witnessed by Scripture, and (3) be fruitfully relevant in our present age. The hermeneutical questions these tests presuppose will be discussed further in chapter 10.

THE MYSTERY OF THE KINGDOM

Jesus spoke a number of parables about the kingdom of God.[5] In a sense these parables are models of the kingdom. Using models is a bit more formal way of dealing with images or metaphors.

As Jesus himself indicated, the kingdom of God is "secret" or a "mystery."[6] Models help to reveal the mystery. This "mysterious" aspect of the kingdom is evident in Jesus' teaching and throughout Scripture. God's reign is a "mystery" in several senses. For example, Scripture speaks of the kingdom as being both present and future. Exactly how this can be true is difficult to understand; it is part of the mystery of the kingdom. But the mystery extends much further. The kingdom is a mystery because it is God's action and yet involves human participation or response, because in some sense its reality is accessible only by faith and because it is in some way bound up with the mystery of the Incarnation. It is, after all, the kingdom *of God,* whose ways are "beyond tracing out" (Rom. 11:33). Further, the kingdom involves the mystery of human history, personality, and culture, none of which is yet fully understood.[7]

Biblical teachings present us with six fundamental *tension points* or *polarities* that are central to the mystery of God's reign. Understanding the kingdom biblically requires recognizing these polarities, and they are keys to the models we will be discussing. We may identify them as follows:

1. *Present versus future.* Jesus said "The kingdom of God is near" (Mark 1:15), but also that we should pray for God's kingdom to come (Matt. 6:10).

2. *Individual versus social.* Jesus said the kingdom is like hidden treasure an individual person might find (Matt. 13:44), but he also said, "Do not be afraid, little flock, for your Father has been pleased to give you the kingdom" (Luke 12:32). He talked about being born again in order to see the kingdom (John 3:3) but also described it as a feast to be shared (Luke 13:29).

3. *Spirit versus matter.* Paul said, "Flesh and blood cannot inherit the kingdom of God" (I Cor. 15:50), and Jesus said, "My kingdom is not of this world" (John 18:36). But Jesus associated himself with the healing and liberation of the Jubilee (Luke 4:18-21) and Revelation speaks of a kingdom in which God's people "will reign on the earth" (Rev. 5:10).

4. *Gradual versus climactic.* Jesus said the kingdom is like grain that grows gradually in a field (Mark 4:26-28). But he also said its coming would be like the midnight cry of the arriving bridegroom (Matt. 25:1-6).

5. *Divine action versus human action.* The kingdom of God is like a returning king who settles accounts (Luke 19:11-27). It is God who rules and reigns (Ps. 99:1-2). Yet, the kingdom is also something we must seek (Matt. 6:33), and Christians can be "fellow workers for the kingdom of God" (Col. 4:11).

6. *The Church's relation to the kingdom;* the tension between seeing the church and the kingdom as essentially the same or as clearly different. Jesus said to the Apostle Peter, "I will give you the keys of the kingdom of heaven" (Matt. 16:19). But he also spoke of the kingdom as future and said that not all those who worshiped him, but only those who did God's will, would enter the kingdom (Matt. 7:21).

Passages that reflect similar tensions might also be cited from the Old Testament.

Any biblical theology of the kingdom will need to wrestle with these polarities. In fact, I would offer the following thesis: Theologies of the kingdom that dissolve these tensions, opting wholly for one side or the other, are to that degree unbiblical. A biblically faithful and biblically useful theology of the kingdom will in some way maintain and live with these tensions.

These six polarities may be illustrated as follows:

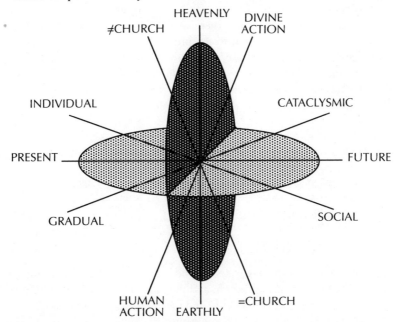

The eight models of the kingdom sketched in the following chapters represent quite different ways of handling these tensions. They show the ways

God's reign may be conceived as we look at the scriptural evidence and how it has in fact been conceived historically.

MODELS OF THE KINGDOM

Constructing models of the kingdom can be a complex business, particularly since we must span two millennia of Christian history. It is desirable to have as few discrete models as possible, and, as we have noted, each must cohere with a kind of internal logic. Yet, the range of models must be broad enough to incorporate the many conceptions of the kingdom that have appeared over time.

Broadly speaking, conceptions of the kingdom may be grouped as *models of future hope, models of present blessing,* or *models of earnest anticipation*—"earnest" here implying not only sincere devotion but also some present experience of what is yet to come. This third group to some degree mediates between the strongly present and future orientations of the first two, holding together the already/not yet tension of the kingdom.

These groupings are too broad, however, to serve as models. Playing out the range of conceptions of God's reign as they are found in history and today in the light of the polarities discussed above, however, yields eight fairly distinct models. In the first, the element of futurity is so decisive that I define it as "future hope"; however, some of the other models also are more oriented to the future than to the present, as we shall see. Likewise, some models reflect more a present and others more an anticipatory sense. In general, the models move from future hope to present realization, but other polarities are involved as well.

The models we will explore, then, are as follows:

1. The kingdom as future hope: the *future* kingdom.
2. The kingdom as inner spiritual experience: the *interior* kingdom.
3. The kingdom as mystical communion: the *heavenly* kingdom.
4. The kingdom as institutional church: the *ecclesiastical* kingdom.
5. The kingdom as countersystem: the *subversive* kingdom.
6. The kingdom as political state: the *theocratic* kingdom.
7. The kingdom as Christianized culture: the *transforming* kingdom.
8. The kingdom as earthly utopia: the *utopian* kingdom.

Each of these models suggests something different about the nature of salvation, the mission of the church, and the meaning of Christian discipleship. Thus each one affects the world and the church in different ways.

This leads to a final comment regarding the models proposed in this book. Are these all really models of the kingdom, or are some of them rather models of spirituality or of the Christian life, unrelated to the question of the kingdom? For in some of the proposed models, kingdom language is scarcely found. My answer is twofold. First, since the kingdom of God is a prominent biblical theme, *some* model of the kingdom is implicit in every understanding of the Christian faith. In other words, a lack of emphasis on the kingdom itself says something about how the kingdom is understood. Second, in any case the kingdom of God is the perspective from which this study is written. To be comprehensive we must look at traditions that have not specifically stressed the kingdom, not just at those that have. In these cases the line of thought is not so much how the kingdom has been understood from this angle, but rather the reverse: What do these perspectives say or imply about the meaning of God's reign? As we shall see, this applies particularly to models two and three, where kingdom language is less frequently or less centrally found.

THE USE OF MODELS

A further word should be added concerning the use of models in theology and specifically in discussing the kingdom of God. A considerable literature on using models in theology has developed over the past three decades, and models are increasingly employed today as a method of theological exploration.[8] It is not necessary to review this literature here. But we may note some special concerns that arise when models are applied to concepts of God's reign or rule.

As Sallie McFague notes, "A model is, in essence, a sustained and systematic metaphor."[9] It is a somewhat formalized way of using metaphorical language to describe or to explore some reality not fully understood. By constructing and exploring models one finds hints of what *may* be true about the hidden reality the models represent. In this sense models help to reveal mystery.

Avery Dulles and others have pointed out the limitations of types and models in theology as well as their usefulness. Dulles writes,

In constructing types on the basis of the expressed views of individual theologians one is moving from the particular to the universal, from the concrete to the abstract, from the actual to the ideal. The type does not exactly correspond to the thought of the theologians whom it allegedly includes. For one thing, the type is simplified; it omits many qualifications and amplifications which the theologians make. Secondly, the type is schematic; it represents a pure position or ideal case from which any given theologian will presumably diverge at certain points, especially if one considers the full output of the individual over a span of years.

As an ideal case, the type may be called a model. That is to say, it is a relatively simple, artificially constructed case which is found to be useful and illuminating for dealing with realities that are more complex and differentiated.[10]

These considerations apply to our discussion of models of the kingdom, for we will be examining views that have been put forth by a number of Christian thinkers. This use of models can be very helpful in theology. "Intelligible as a unit, each model can readily be grasped holistically, in such a manner that the details easily fall into place."[11] Well-constructed models are simple and clear enough to be grasped more or less intuitively; yet they have a logical or, better, an analogical relation to the larger reality being investigated.

Dulles suggests that when working with types or models it is best to employ "a relatively small number of types, all of which can be kept simultaneously in mind. The typology will be more successful if the types are sharply delineated, so that their differences are evident, and if each is capable of being characterized by a single orientation or metaphor that gives the key to the positions taken on a large number of questions."[12] The models proposed here have been developed with these considerations in mind.

It is well, then, to keep two points in mind in using models. First, each model is "ideal" or "synthetic" in the sense that its "pure" form may not actually be found in history. A model is to some degree an intentional abstraction from reality in order to clarify issues.

Second, models may not be mutually exclusive. To some degree various models balance or supplement each other. On the other hand, some pairs of models are virtual opposites so that to embrace one seems to require rejecting the other. In his empirical study of congregational models, James Hopewell discovered that typically a congregation exemplifies one primary model and one or two secondary ones, rejecting the polar opposite of the primary model. Although his typology has only four basic models, something similar happens, I think, with models of the kingdom. Seldom does a person or movement affirm or embody one model of the kingdom exclusively. Yet generally, one model is primary, even though it may be supplemented by others, and the model perceived to be the opposite of the primary one is rejected.[13]

We may think of a set of models as forming a continuum, or perhaps multidimensional continua, with some models more complementary and others more in conflict with their opposites (as the illustration above indicates). A continuum suggests, theoretically, the possibility of an infinite number of models. But it is more useful to work with relatively few models, which can be clearly distinguished and have their own internal logic, rather than with many, which may too greatly overlap or shade into each other. I am, however, attempting to be comprehensive—that is, to include all major models of the kingdom. The models proposed amount to a framework that, at least in theory, can embrace the range of possible conceptions of God's reign. The idea of a continuum is a reminder, however, that from certain angles some views of the kingdom do overlap or approximate others.

One might classify views of the kingdom in a variety of ways.[14] Obvious possibilities would be to search out differing understandings of God's reign in Scripture or to compare how the kingdom has been understood at different periods in history or in different theological traditions. These approaches have, in fact, been taken by various authors, and I have drawn on these. To some extent their work has made mine possible.[15]

Quite different approaches to the kingdom might be organized around a specific issue or theological concern—for example, understandings of Jesus Christ, sociopolitical questions, the environment, or missions.[16] Diverse conceptions of the kingdom might say rather different things concerning the way Christians should treat the environment, for instance, or what the role of the church in society should be. We will examine some of these issues in passing, but the overall framework is more inclusive.

The approach used here draws on Scripture and on history but is more comprehensive and synthetic than either a biblical or a strictly historical examination would be. The reason for this is pragmatic: I am seeking to be as practical as possible in sorting out different kingdom views. It seems to me that there is only a relatively small number of really fundamental ways of conceiving the kingdom of God—at least up to our time in history. The number of possible "root metaphors" for the kingdom (itself a metaphor) seems to be finite, partly because the biblical sources and the historical record are finite. One can cut the pie in only so many ways and still have pieces large enough to be grasped and to be nourishing.

I am not arguing that this finite number of major models is eight, or that all possible models are encompassed here. In fact, the classification I propose is an invitation to dialogue. I will be grateful if this book stimulates further discussion that will make the concept and the reality of God's reign more useful today as global Christianity enters its third millennium.

It is this consideration—the reality of what Walbert Bühlmann calls "the Third Church"—that makes this discussion particularly timely. Noting that the Christian church is now statistically universal as never before and that its numerical center of gravity has shifted from the northern to the southern hemisphere, Bühlmann says, "The Third Church is approaching, church of the Third World but also church of the third millennium."[17] The church has never before faced today's challenge: being empirically a world community of diverse traditions and cultures, confronting a new world awareness and emerging global economy, and needing a theology that is truly universal and ecological. It is because of this challenge that I am seeking to be as comprehensive and inclusive as possible in presenting a set of models. In this sense my approach is like H. Richard Niebuhr's in *Christ and Culture*.[18]

I have attempted to work out a typology into which fall, without being forced, all theologies of the kingdom that have significantly shaped the church and human history.

Because of this practical focus, I am less concerned here with technical theological discussions than with how the kingdom has been understood popularly in the church and by key leaders who have shaped history. The kingdom of God is a primary metaphor by which Christians have sought to understand what it means to believe in Christ and through him to be related to God and the world. Thus this book is not primarily a history or analysis of the *theological interpretation* of the kingdom of God, though of course the discussion is theological. Rather, the book shows how the kingdom has been understood, especially by those who have sought to live the life of the kingdom. I am interested not so much in discussions of theologians who see the kingdom as one among many topics to be explored as I am in those people in history who have been radically committed to God's reign, believing it held the central meaning of their lives as Christian believers and as actors in the human drama. This focus governs to a large extent the choice of writers and sources cited.

KINGDOM: AN OUTDATED MODEL?

"Kingdom of God" is itself a model, a metaphor for understanding the world and God's relation to it. Some would say, in fact, that this is the primary model of salvation introduced by Jesus. It is a highly symbolic representation that immediately suggests a number of things about God and God's relationship to the world.

We need to ask, however, whether such a "monarchical model" is appropriate today. Would we be better off without it? Some have argued strongly against such a model, not so much because monarchy itself is viewed as outmoded but because of the claim that "traditional imperialistic imagery for God is opposed to life, its continuation and fulfillment" because it unduly shifts responsibility from human beings to God.[19] If this claim is true, then we should abandon the monarchical model altogether. Rather than exploring models of the kingdom, we should look for other models that don't carry this oppressive danger.

Two things must be borne in mind, however. The first is fairly obvious: The kingdom of God is a biblical theme and, therefore, an inherent part of the Christian tradition. If one believes, as I do, that theology is genuinely Christian only to the extent that it is biblical, then thinking Christians have to deal with God's reign carefully and responsibly. Certainly one cannot understand church history without grasping the role the kingdom concept has played. It may very well be, of course, that this is not a particularly helpful concept for today. Perhaps other biblical themes should now become prominent. Some similar line of thought may have been at work in the Apostle Paul's mind, for he apparently chose (at times) to stress other images, such as the "economy" (*oikonomia*) of God. We may return more helpfully to this question later after examining the various kingdom models discussed below.

My second response concerns the nature of models themselves. As already suggested, no one model is fully adequate, and models must be compared with and perhaps balanced by other models. Especially is this true when we are dealing with the wealth and breadth of biblical themes. If we respond negatively to the idea of the kingdom of God, this is probably because of history's negative experiences with kings and kingdoms (as we today may assess them) and because of aversion to the idea of dominance/subservience, which king and kingdom imply.

The key question, however, if we are speaking biblically, is this: What kind of king is God? Here our models of God are crucial. If God is loving, caring, nurturing, longsuffering, and faithful, then it is hard to view God's sovereign rule in a negative light, unless one objects to notions of power and authority altogether. If God is not only King but also Shepherd, Father, Mother, and Gardener (all biblical images) then these images radically condition how the kingdom of God is to be understood. Those who oppose "kingdom of God" as oppressive seem to assume that every form of rulership is *necessarily* oppressive, or that their proposed alternatives are inherently positive or nonoppressive. But the conclusion does not necessarily follow.[20]

The problem is not with the image of kingdom itself. Rather it is the failure to balance "imperial" and patriarchal images with other biblical images of God and salvation. Part of the problem is the church's failure to take seriously enough the implications of its own affirmation that God is Trinity.[21] I would argue for an inclusive view of biblical images of God and salvation, not a pendulum swing away from language or metaphors that may be less palatable today. To reject the language of kingdom because kings may be oppressive is something like rejecting the language of motherhood because some mothers may abuse or neglect their children.

For all his stress on love, kindness, and servanthood, Jesus himself spoke much about the kingdom of God. But typically he called God "Father," not "King." The reign of God is not the rule of a tyrant. Rather it is the providential care of a loving and compassionate parent (even though this is not the way it has often been portrayed).

But there is another important point here. The Bible does speak of God as Judge, conquering King, and holy Fire. It speaks of the wrath and righteous anger of God. However unpopular such conceptions of God may be today, they are biblical.[22] And they raise an important question: Can we simply abandon such understandings as outmoded or oppressive? Or do they in fact tell us something essential about the mystery of God, something that, if lost, makes us less capable of knowing God fully and of really being God's people on earth today? One value (some would say liability) of the kingdom theme is that it may guard against a too humanistic or pantheistic view of God.

My position is that the kingdom deserves attention partly because it *is* a key biblical theme and partly because of the age we live in. The kingdom of God is a powerful symbol that can have fresh fruitfulness today. I believe also that the kingdom is more than a theoretical construct; it is ontologically based in the fact that God, however humanly understood, created the universe and is sovereign within and "over" all creation. The metaphor of the kingdom tells us that God is distinguishable from but not unrelated to the created order and that in fundamental ways God bears a relationship of power and authority toward all God has made. Divergent ways of conceiving the kingdom, however, yield quite different understandings for our lives in relationship to God and others and the world.

I would leave open, however, the question of whether other ways of speaking about God's sovereignty, power, and purpose may be more useful than "kingdom of God" as we move toward a new century. What appropriate images or metaphors will emerge? Tony Campolo suggests that *The Kingdom of God Is a Party.*[23] Family, community, "kindom of God," and other models have been suggested. I would not be surprised to see "kingdom of God" language fade and other terms and metaphors come to the fore, but the fundamental issues will remain. In chapter 11, I briefly explore some new alternatives, drawing on themes of *ecology* and *drama*.

To assess such suggestions intelligently, however, we must first explore the range of options already available to us.

2 MODEL ONE: THE KINGDOM AS FUTURE HOPE

My kingdom is not of this world. (John 18:36)

PERHAPS MORE than anything else, the kingdom of God has been for Christians a future hope. It has been a pointer beyond this life to something more ultimate and complete—not mere spiritual survival only but a final cosmic reconciliation. This is the Future Kingdom, viewed either as that final cosmic reconciliation itself or as a millennial reign preceding the ultimate summation of all things. A primary image in this model is that of "a new heaven and a new earth."

The early church experienced the "already" of the kingdom in Jesus' own presence and his announcement that the kingdom of God was at hand and in the presence of the Holy Spirit after Pentecost. But the early Christians experienced its "not yet" aspect in the promise of Jesus' return and in his words about an endtime that had not yet arrived. Jesus' parables likewise speak of a king or landowner who is absent now but will return and settle accounts in the future. That this sense of initial fulfillment but ultimate climax was present in the church from the beginning is seen in Peter's sermon recorded in Acts 3:

> Repent, then, and turn to God, so that your sins may be wiped out, that times of refreshing may come from the Lord, and that he may send the Christ, who has been appointed for you—even Jesus. He must remain in heaven until the time comes for God to restore everything, as he promised long ago through his holy prophets. (Acts 3:19-21)

The Christian faith is both present- and future-oriented. It is *historical*—grounded in God's action in the past and understanding the present in terms of both past history and future hope. This element of future hope has always been present in the church, though not always accented. Since Scripture presents this hope largely in terms of the kingdom of God, the church has understood that whatever else the kingdom may be, it represents a fundamental hope for the future.

This persistent and fundamental link between God's kingdom and future blessing or reconciliation makes it appropriate to consider the Future Kingdom as our first model. Though it occurs in a variety of forms, it is marked by at least four basic features. The first is, of course, the future focus; futurity is the key to this conception of God's reign. The primary present meaning of the kingdom is the hope it offers for finally putting to rights all that is wrong in the world. Thus this is a model of both ultimate judgment and ultimate reconciliation.

This expectation of final judgment is a second key feature of this model. The coming of the kingdom means not merely the end of history or the giving of rewards. It will really be a summing up, a cosmic reconciliation and a final settling of the score regarding all the evils and injustices of history. This may include the idea that the End is not merely the overcoming of all the evil caused by the Fall but also a form of new creation, something greater or more glorious than the state of the cosmos before the Fall. In John Wesley's view, for example: "The whole brute creation will then undoubtedly be restored, not only to the vigour, strength, and swiftness which they had at their creation, but to a far higher degree of each than they ever enjoyed. They will be restored, not only to that measure of understanding which they had in paradise, but to a degree of it as much higher than that as the understanding of an elephant is beyond that of a worm."[1] "For all the earth shall then be a more beautiful paradise than Adam ever saw"; humankind will enjoy "an unmixed state of holiness and happiness far superior to that which Adam enjoyed in paradise."[2]

Another mark of this model is a general pessimism concerning the present order. Since we live in a fallen, ruined world that bears in every area the marks of the Fall, there is no hope for the world short of the second coming of Christ. For the present, Christians can at best serve as a sort of brake on the world's downhill slide. As salt, Christians act as a preservative against the world's decay; as light, they help to illuminate the darkness. But there is no fundamental hope for the transformation of the present social order.

A final characteristic of this model is its emphasis on the second coming of Jesus Christ. New Testament passages about Jesus' return and Old Testament predictions about the Day of the Lord are particularly stressed. The return of Christ is the church's "blessed hope" (Tit. 2:13). A classic text here is Matthew 24, in which Jesus speaks of the signs of "the end of the age" and of "the coming of the Son of Man" and says that "this gospel of the kingdom will be preached in the whole world as a testimony to all nations, and then the end will come" (Matt. 24:14; other passages of similar importance are Luke 12:35-40; 17:20-37; 21:5-36; Acts 1:11; and I Thess. 4:13-18).[3]

There are, of course, many Old Testament prophecies concerning a coming judgment and many references in the Psalms and elsewhere to God's rule over all things. This model stresses passages that speak of final judgment and reconciliation, such as Isaiah 11; 24:21-23; the promise of "new heavens and a new earth" in Isaiah 65:17 and 66:22; and similar promises in writings of the other prophets.

A related biblical theme is that of the kingdom as an inheritance. New Testament passages—such as James 2:5, which says God has chosen the poor "to inherit the kingdom he promised those who love him," and Colossians 1:12 which speaks of "the inheritance of the saints in the kingdom of light"—draw on the theme of inheritance found in the Hebrew Scriptures.[4]

EXPLORING THE MODEL

In examining this and subsequent models of the kingdom, it will be useful to ask a few key questions. These questions concern the scope, agency, and evidence of the kingdom, as well as its participants or beneficiaries, its opponents, and its final goal. Raising these issues will help us to understand the models and how they relate to each other.

The Future Kingdom model sees God reigning eternally over the entire cosmos, but primarily in a spiritual sense or within a spiritual realm. At some point in the future, God's reign will be fully manifest on earth as well as in heaven. It is God and God alone who reigns; in this model there is little place for human agency in building or manifesting the kingdom. God (primarily as Jesus Christ or the Holy Spirit) now rules secretly in the hearts of believers, whose response is to be one of faith, devotion, and obedience within the limited sphere of their lives. There is little expectation of a public, social-oriented role for Christians or for the church that contributes anything to the kingdom of God.

In this model the signs of the kingdom are primarily apocalyptic and miraculous. The kingdom is opposed by satanic forces and by the Antichrist, however that figure may be understood. The power of the kingdom may be demonstrated in power encounters between divine and demonic forces. Social and political events may be seen as "signs"—not so much as signs of the kingdom itself but as "signs of the times"—that is, signs of the approaching Apocalypse, which will usher in the millennium or the kingdom in its fullness. The participants in and beneficiaries of the kingdom are true Christians now and ultimately all those who accept Jesus Christ as Savior and Lord. Some advocates of this model, following the Apostle Paul in Romans 10, make a point of including the Jewish race in the final culmination of the kingdom.

The final goal in the Future Kingdom model is the judgment of evil and the reconciliation of all things, including the reconciling or conjoining of the material and spiritual realms in a new heaven and new earth. It is thus the final demonstration of the justice, love, and power of God in a universe cleansed from all evil and discord and joining in the praise of God. The vision of the New Jerusalem in Revelation 21 and 22 is the supreme picture of what the finally established kingdom of God will mean.

THE MODEL IN HISTORY

This view of the kingdom has been a primary one throughout much of church history. Most scholars agree that the Future Kingdom was the commonly accepted view in the church during the first two centuries, either as a future earthly reign of Christ or as the perfect reign of God in heaven following the Last Judgment. The *Didache* (c. A.D. 150) contains the prayer, "Let your Church be brought together from the ends of the earth into your Kingdom"; "Make it holy, 'and gather' it 'together from the four winds' into your Kingdom which you have made ready for it."[5] Though other views began to emerge during the third century, and especially in the fourth century when Christianity was officially recognized by the Roman Empire, the accent of the kingdom as future was the basic view throughout the early period. The realization of this future hope might be seen as near or far. Millenarian views tend to see the ultimate inbreaking of the future as being near at hand, whereas other views see the culmination as coming in a more distant future.

As time passed Christians had to deal with the fact that Jesus did not immediately return to establish the kingdom in its fullness. This did not necessarily mean, however, a diminishing of the kingdom hope in the church. Jaroslav Pelikan notes that "one looks in vain for proof of a bitter disappointment over the postponement of the parousia or of a shattering of the early Christian communities by the delay of the Lord's return. What the texts do suggest is a shift within the polarity of already/not yet and a great variety of solutions to the exegetical and theological difficulties caused by such a shift."[6] Many believed in a literal millennial reign of Christ on earth, based on Revelation 20:1-10. As Pelikan notes, however, the sources provide "striking evidence not only that the millenarian hope continued in the church after the apostolic age, but also that, probably from the beginning, it stood in tension with other descriptions of the reign of Christ, which were not as privy to the details of the timetable for this reign."[7] The millennial understanding of the future kingdom was simply one permissible view among others.

In his important work *Against Heresies,* Irenaeus (c. 115–c. 202), bishop of Lyons, sees all of history as being renewed or "recapitulated" in Jesus Christ.[8] This shapes his view of the kingdom of God, which is one of ultimate restoration and renewal. Drawing especially on Romans 8 and on God's promise of land to Abraham, Irenaeus writes that Christians will inherit the kingdom not just in a spiritual sense but literally, within "this created order, then made new," following the resurrection of the righteous and "the appearance of God." It is right and just "that in the same order in which they were put to death for the love of God they should again be made alive and that in the same order in which they suffered bondage they should reign." Creation will be "restored to its pristine state"; the meek will inherit the earth. "These things are [to be] in the times of the Kingdom, that is, on the seventh day," when God rested, "when the just rising from the dead, will reign, when the created order will be made new and set free, and will produce an abundance of all kinds of food, from the dew of heaven and the fertility of the earth."[9] So Irenaeus writes, "Neither the substance nor the essence of the created order vanishes away, for he is true and faithful who established it, but the pattern of this world passes away, that is, the things in which the transgression took place, since in them man has grown old."[10]

Here the kingdom is future but will be a literal fulfillment of the biblical kingdom promises, though following the resurrection and a fundamental renewal or transformation of the created order. This is a certain hope of a kingdom yet to come.

Tertullian (c. A.D. 160–c. 225) provides a particularly interesting study of Christian understandings of the kingdom as Christianity progressed through the third century. Tertullian, an accomplished scholar and able apologist for the faith, was troubled by what he saw as growing moral laxity in the church. His concern with the kingdom was not merely theological and apologetic. He pointed to its practical meaning in the light of the challenges Christians were facing in his day.

Toward the end of his life Tertullian became a part of the New Prophecy movement, later known as Montanism. Whether Montanism influenced his views of the kingdom, or conversely whether he influenced Montanist eschatology, is a disputed question. In any case it is clear that the Montanist movement saw the kingdom of God primarily as a future hope. With their strong emphasis on prophecy and new revelations through the Spirit, however, Montanists expected this hope to be realized soon. They seem to have been particularly attracted to the writings of the Apostle John and apparently expected that the New Jerusalem would descend from heaven near the town of Pepuza in Phrygia (an area associated with John's later ministry and apparently Montanus's home area).

In summarizing the creed, Tertullian says the Word of God was incarnated in Jesus Christ, who "preached the new law and the new promise of the kingdom of heaven" and who "will come with glory to take the saints to the enjoyment of everlasting life and of the heavenly promises" and to judge the wicked.[11] "We do confess that a kingdom is promised to us upon the earth," says Tertullian, "although before heaven, only in another state of existence; inasmuch as it will be after the resurrection for a thousand years in the divinely-built city of Jerusalem, 'let down from heaven.'"[12] He explains:

> Of the heavenly kingdom this is the process. After its thousand years are over, within which period is completed the resurrection of the saints, who rise sooner or later according to their deserts, there will ensue the destruction of the world and the conflagration of all things at the judgment: we shall then be changed in a moment into the substance of angels, even by the investiture of an incorruptible nature, and so be removed to that kingdom in heaven of which we have now been treating.[13]

Christians now enjoy heavenly blessings even as they deny themselves earthly ones for the sake of the kingdom. But in the millennium they will enjoy "also earthly blessings" in the fulfillment of Jesus' words about seeking the kingdom in Matthew 6:33.[14]

Tertullian believed God reigned over all but also that Satan was active in the world and that conditions were getting worse and the catastrophe of the last days was at hand. Christians are pilgrims expecting the return of Christ. Their hope is their resurrection and the coming of the eternal kingdom. Pelikan suggests that Tertullian had a sort of bipolar eschatology in which the kingdom was both present and future, but the primary emphasis was on the future.[15]

Though with somewhat different features because of changed historical and cultural contexts, this futurist model of the kingdom has had currency throughout much of church history. It was certainly one of the principal streams of Christian thought and expectation in Western medieval Christendom (though often overshadowed by the model of the kingdom as institutional church). This view has been popular especially during troubled or seemingly apocalyptic times, such as periods of plague or war.

The trinitarian dispensationalism of Joachim of Fiore (c. A.D. 1135–1202) was a particularly influential and controversial form of this model. Joachim was the abbot of an obscure Cistercian monastery. Around the age of fifty he received spiritual insights through which he elaborated views on the relationship between the two Testaments, the meaning of the Trinity, and the nature of history. Later he founded his own Order of St. John (San Giovanni) at Fiore in a remote mountain plateau in Calabria.

Joachim's writings had immense influence both in his own day and since. Jürgen Moltmann observes, "Ever since the middle ages, there is hardly anyone who has influenced European movements for liberty in church, state and culture more profoundly than this twelfth-century Cistercian abbot from Calabria, who believed that in his vision he had penetrated the concordance of the Old and New Testaments, and the mystery of the Book of Revelation."[16] Moltmann sees echoes of Joachim's theory of the ages of history even in Karl Marx.[17] Franklin Littell notes, "The radical Franciscans used the intellectual weaponry of Joachim against the papacy, and from that time there has flowed an underground river of radical eschatology in the West. In modern times it has surfaced repeatedly among persons and movements who have no knowledge of its origin, e.g., in Cotton Mather and his Age of the Triumph of the Eternal Gospel, in Karl Marx and his idea of the withering away of the state."[18]

The key to Joachim's influence is the appeal of his theory of history in its general concept rather than in its specific details. He has been called the first systematic thinker about the nature and meaning of history. Working with patterns of twos and threes, and sevens and twelves, Joachim elaborated a theory of three great ages of history, corresponding to the persons of the Trinity. He wrote:

> The First Age of the world began with Adam, flowered from Abraham, and was consummated in Christ. The Second began with Oziah, flowered from Zachary, the father of John the Baptist, and will receive its consummation in these times. The Third Age, taking its beginning from St. Benedict, began to bring forth fruit in the twenty-second generation, and is itself to be consummated in the consummation of the world. The First Age, in which the married state was illustrious, is ascribed to the Father in the personal aspect of the [Trinitaran] mystery. The Second, in which the clerical state in the tribe of Juda was illustrious, is ascribed to the Son; the Third, in which the monastic state is illustrious, is ascribed to the Holy Spirit.[19]

The Second Age would last for forty-two generations of about thirty years each; thus the Third Age of the Spirit would begin about A.D. 1260 (though Joachim himself set no date). New religious orders would arise in this Third Age that would convert the world and bring about a truly spiritual church (*ecclesia spiritualis*). Understandably, many Franciscans and Dominicans, whose orders began about this time, saw in themselves the beginning fulfillment of Joachim's prophecy—as did many others who hoped for renewal in the church and the coming of the kingdom.

Few of these ideas were themselves new. Joachim worked with a common stock of ideas, including, obviously, biblical history and apocalyptic. His genius lay in combining two eschatological traditions: that of seven ages of history corresponding to the six days of creation and a final day of rest, and the Cappadocian tradition, which saw God's kingdom as having somewhat different modes in history corresponding to the different Persons of the Trinity. "Joachim's great idea was to identify the seventh day of world history with the kingdom of the Spirit. The great 'sabbath' of history, before the end of the world, and the kingdom of the Spirit mean the same thing."[20] Thus Joachim wrote:

> The mysteries of Holy Scripture point us to three orders (states, or conditions) of the world: to the first, in which we were under the Law; to the second, in which we are under grace; to the third, which we already imminently expect, and in which we shall be under a yet more abundant grace. . . .
>
> The first condition is in the bondage of slaves, the second in the bondage of sons, the third in liberty.[21]

Joachim's conception is dynamic rather than static, for history is tied up in the mystery of the Trinity. The stages of history are interrelated so that each is implicit in the others and the earlier stages foreshadow the later ones. Moltmann suggests that Joachim's views in fact imply four stages: "Joachim interpreted the history of the kingdom in trinitarian terms, and the consummation of the kingdom in eschatological ones. This is to say he in fact developed a doctrine of *four* kingdoms: the kingdoms of the Father, the Son and the Spirit will be consummated in the triune God's kingdom of glory. This fact is often overlooked."[22] This view is more historically potent than that of orthodox Protestantism, Moltmann argues, because Protestantism traditionally has spoken only of the kingdom of nature and the kingdom of grace within history, either placing the kingdom of the Spirit beyond history or in effect making it synonymous with the kingdom of the Son (the kingdom of grace). In Moltmann's view, this is not a fully Trinitarian understanding of the kingdom and undercuts much of the charismatic and liberating dynamic of God's reign.

This raises the question of whether Joachim's views really represent the Future Kingdom model. This model does not, however, necessarily put the fullness of the kingdom beyond history, but only in the future. Joachim's views were attractive in large measure because he saw this future as very near, and in fact as foreshadowed in current events. The mainline view also expected a final, future kingdom, but still a long way off. With his emphasis on connected but cumulative history, Joachim fired eschatological expectations in a way that implicitly criticized the church of his time. As Bernard McGinn notes, Joachim's "concept of the third age . . . was a radical critique of the thirteenth century church."[23] His "stress on the domination of the spiritual and the charismatic over the institutional and rational in the future church was diametrically opposed to the forces that triumphed during the thirteenth century."[24] The power of Joachim's views was his belief that "God would initiate the age of the Holy Spirit, the perfection of the divine action *within history*. Only after the third age would come the final tribulation and the sabbath rest of eternity."[25]

Joachim's views illustrate the Future Kingdom model, though in a unique way and with the particular fascination and appeal that dispensational theories always have. Since he expected the Age of the Spirit before Christ's Second Coming, his eschatology is technically postmillennial, in contrast to most varieties of the Future Kingdom model. In this sense Joachim's views have certain linkages with models seven and eight, which see the kingdom now at work in society even though in some sense still future. His views also share with these models an optimism that is often absent from futurist models.

Perhaps Joachim is best seen as an illustration of the way the future kingdom model can be employed to critique the church and raise strong hope for imminent renewal through the power of the Spirit. He represents the Future Kingdom model in his accent on the future; yet, he transcends the model in ways that ultimately made him a key source for yet more radical and revolutionary kingdom conceptions.

As we have seen, the defining mark of this first model is its stress on a final reconciliation or summing up, a "new heaven and new earth," which will come in the future. The kingdom is more future hope than it is present experience, whether as inner spiritual reality or ecclesiastical embodiment. In Protestantism God's kingdom has for the most part been understood as a future hope, but with more or less stress as well on the *present* spiritual/mystical or ecclesiastical realization of the kingdom. In other words, the future element has nearly always been present as a foundation or substratum but at times has been overshadowed by other accents, giving rise to other models. The kingdom as future hope has been the dominant model only at those times or among those groups where futurity was the element that shaped all the others.

John Wesley and eighteenth-century Methodism represent this model to the degree that Wesley anticipated a final kingdom of glory, a time of cosmic reconciliation, the "restitution of all things" (Acts 3:21 KJV) when all the great Old Testament promises of *shalom* would be fulfilled. In some of his sermons (such as "The General Deliverance" and "The New Creation") Wesley writes of that final reconciliation in ways that are quite similar to Irenaeus's views, noted above. In his *Explanatory Notes Upon the New Testament,* Wesley took over the postmillennial framework of the German Pietist J. A. Bengel in his notes on Revelation. Yet, Wesley's primary focus was not on the future kingdom of glory but on the present kingdom of grace; not so much on the future as on the present experience of Christ reigning in the heart and within the believing community. It will be more appropriate, therefore, to discuss Wesley's views under model two, the Inner Kingdom.

The late nineteenth century was a time of accenting the future model, particularly in conservative sectors of Protestantism in the United States and Europe. In part this was a reaction to the times and to the beginning of the rise of the social gospel. One can trace the resurgence of this model in a somewhat apocalyptic form in the events leading up to the birth of Pentecostalism at the turn of the century and, in a different way, in the rise of Protestant Fundamentalism with its dispensational framework.

Pentecostalism represents probably the most extensive embodiment of this model in the twentieth century. This is particularly significant in the light of the dramatic growth of the Pentecostal and Charismatic movements worldwide over the past several decades. Pentecostalism arose in part out of a heightened expectation of the imminent inbreaking of a new age of the Spirit. As Donald Dayton and others have shown, the Pentecostal Movement was the fruit of a gradual shift in emphasis (primarily in the American Holiness Movement) from Jesus Christ to the Holy Spirit, from process to crisis, and from a post- to a premillennial understanding of the kingdom.[26] Robert Mapes Anderson writes: "By the turn of the century most Holiness people were agreed on the imminent, premillennial, apocalyptic Second Coming of Christ, preceded by a great world-wide revival of Pentecostal dimensions."[27] Thus tongues speaking, when it appeared at the turn of the century, was not just the sign of the fullness of the Spirit. It was also a sign of the endtimes; of the imminence of the Second Coming and God's reign on earth.

The Future Kingdom model is more characteristic of Pentecostalism, however, than it is of Charismatic Christianity, which grew from it. In fact, a significant point of difference between these two movements, which otherwise obviously have much in common, can be seen here. Presumably socioeconomic factors are part of the story. In general the Charismatic Movement has been more middle class than Pentecostalism has been. As has often been noted, apocalyptic and future-oriented visions of the Christian hope frequently arise among the poor or the nearly poor. In the Charismatic Movement the gifts of the Spirit are seen as useful for the vitality of the church and for personal spiritual growth and witness but are felt to have much less eschatological significance than was true in early Pentecostalism.

A MILLENNIAL KINGDOM?

The future kingdom, as we have seen, may be understood as a thousand-year reign of Christ on earth (millennialism or chiliasm, from the Roman and Greek words for "thousand") or in other ways. Revelation 20 speaks of Satan's being bound and of Christian martyrs coming to life and reigning with Christ: "The second death has no power over them, but they will be priests of God and of Christ and will reign with him for a thousand years" (Rev. 20:6). The question of millennialism also raises issues concerning social movements of the poor and possible Christian origins of social revolt. Much has been written on these questions from differing perspectives. A classic study is Norman Cohn's *Pursuit of the Millennium.*[28] Cohn shows how millennial movements have risen repeatedly in church history, sometimes straining or ripping the social fabric.

Millennialism raises a host of other issues as well. One of these is the question of utopian visions which seek to embody the kingdom of God in present-day society. As we shall see, such visions actually introduce another model: the kingdom as earthly utopia (model eight in our discussion). In one sense the utopian model represents the farthest extreme from the vision of the kingdom as future hope, but in another sense it is a near neighbor. We may imagine the continuum of models curving into a circle so that the two extremes finally meet. We shall pursue this further in chapter 9.

Whether Jesus Christ will return to inaugurate the millennium (premillennialism) or climactically at its end (postmillennialism) has been a central issue in modern discussions about the meaning of Jesus' thousand-year reign. Of the various millennial views, however, premillennialism seems best to fit the Future Kingdom model because of its insistence that the kingdom cannot come in fullness until the cataclysmic event of the Second Coming. Other views are more continuous with present history and thus more likely to see the kingdom as already present in the world in at least some anticipatory sense.

It would be misleading, however, to think of the Future Kingdom model as necessarily implying millennialism, for there can be millennial and non-millennial views of the kingdom as future hope. The thousand-year reign referred to in Revelation 20 may be understood literally or symbolically or simply disregarded. The promise of the kingdom remains a central hope for the future, even if it is understood in a more general, less detailed, or more distant sense.

In Pentecostal and Charismatic versions of this model, future hope becomes present experience in a partial sense through the gifts and powers of the Holy Spirit. This was true as well for Montanism and other versions of this model that put particular stress on the Spirit.

Recent decades have seen a new interest in the kingdom of God within Evangelical Protestantism in the United States. This traces in part to Evangelicalism's struggles with the constricting framework of Fundamentalist dispensationalism as Evangelicalism emerged in the 1940s and 1950s. Especially influential have been the writings of George Eldon Ladd (1911–82), who was professor of biblical theology at Fuller Theological Seminary in California. Noting "a growing consensus in New Testament scholarship that the Kingdom of God is in some sense both present and future," Ladd articulated a biblical kingdom theology that was distinct from the rigid dispensationalism of Fundamentalism, on the one hand, and from more liberal "realized" and "consistent eschatology" views on the other.[29] He attempted to hold together the present/future polarity in a way that was true to the New Testament documents. It would be fair to say that Ladd's primary model is the Future Kingdom, but he also speaks of the kingdom as "a present spiritual reality" and "a realm into which the followers of Jesus Christ have [already] entered."[30]

Ladd's books have been very influential within some Charismatic and Evangelical renewal circles in recent years. A particularly significant example is John Wimber and the Vineyard Movement. Beginning in the early 1980s, Wimber, pastor of a small congregation with Quaker roots in the Los Angeles area, began to emphasize healing and other "signs and wonders" as these were becoming manifest in his congregation. In 1981 he teamed up with C. Peter Wagner at Fuller Theological Seminary to teach what became a controversial but popular course, "Signs and Wonders and Church Growth." By 1985 Wimber's congregation had changed its name to "Vineyard," had grown to 5000 members, and had founded some 120 other Vineyard congregations. As James Coggins and Paul Hiebert note, "Many of these were already established independent congregations or congregations belonging to another denomination which joined the Vineyard bandwagon in the expectation of experiencing revival."[31]

The Vineyard Movement continues to grow, partly through Signs and Wonders Seminars held across the United States and around the world. Established as the Association of Vineyard Churches in 1986, the group now has more than two hundred congregations in North America and is sending missionaries to other countries. The goal is to plant up to ten thousand Vineyard congregations.[32] Its transition from a loose network of conferences and informal contacts into a denomination resembles the process one hundred years earlier by which individuals and regional associations that were part of the Holiness Movement coalesced to form several new Wesleyan Holiness denominations (of which today the Church of the Nazarene has become the largest). The Vineyard is broadly a part of Charismatic Christianity but is developing a distinct identity and is sometimes seen as a part of a "Third Wave" of the Spirit, in distinction from Pentecostalism and the Charismatic Movement.

Wimber takes the kingdom of God as his starting point in developing his message of "signs and wonders" and "power evangelism." Christians experience the gifts and power of the Holy Spirit so that they may both proclaim and *demonstrate* the reality of the kingdom. Wimber writes, "I found a key for effective evangelism: combining the proclamation with the demonstration of the gospel" through the gifts of the Spirit.[33] Further, he found in Ladd's writings the theological basis for integrating his concern with evangelism, the power of the Spirit, and church growth. He concluded that Ladd's "work on the kingdom of God formed a theological basis for power evangelism."[34]

In Wimber's view, Christians are now involved in "cosmic warfare" between the kingdom of God and the kingdom of Satan. The church, he says, is

> thrust into the middle of a battle with Satan: it's a tug-of-war and the prize is the souls of men and women. Satan's captivity of men and women has many facets, but denying them final salvation is his primary goal. But there are other types of dominion: bondage to sin, physical and emotional problems, social disruption, and demonic affliction.
>
> Our mission is to rescue those who have been taken captive as a result of Adam's fall.[35]

Wimber follows Peter Wagner in distinguishing between "social" and "personal" signs of the kingdom. "Social signs" apply to society as a whole and center in the Jubilee proclamation of good news to the poor and liberty to the oppressed, whereas "personal signs"—such as miracles, healings, and speaking in tongues—relate to specific individuals and are attention getters for the sake of evangelism, while also pointing ahead to the kingdom. "Miracles are a foreshadowing and promise of coming universal redemption and the fullness of the kingdom," says Wimber.[36] By "signs and wonders" Wimber means primarily the "personal signs" of the kingdom. This view of kingdom signs tends to narrow the focus of the church's present mission to personal salvation. It provides scant theological basis for the power of the Spirit in the transformation of society except through individual conversion.

Does Wimber understand the kingdom primarily as future hope? Yes and no. The element of futurity is prominent and foundational, but he also stresses present manifestations of kingdom power, as do many charismatics. Though the kingdom is essentially future, we experience its power now through conversion and the signs and wonders of the Spirit. The Vineyard Movement thus represents a variation of the classical Future Kingdom model but with a strong emphasis on present manifestations of the power of the Spirit, particularly for the sake of evangelism. In its insistence that the power and gifts of the Spirit are for today it represents a conscious critique of dispensational views that see such manifestations as confined to the early church and the future kingdom. Wimber and the Vineyard constitute a fresh emphasis on the kingdom of God and on the present inbreaking of kingdom power. Their primary model is the kingdom as future hope, but that hope is also present in spiritual experience (model two) and a shared communion as Christians worship and fellowship together (model three).

ASSESSING THE MODEL

What are the values and liabilities of this model? By way of critique, we may make three observations. First, this model tends to be pessimistic regarding the present order—so much so that it may undercut confidence in the power of God's grace in the world and induce an unbiblical passivity. With the present/future polarity tilted strongly toward the future, Christians tend to see their calling as one of waiting patiently for the kingdom or as solely one of working to rescue souls from this passing world for eternal life in the world to come. This view can make Christians indifferent to or fatalistic about social problems that could be changed. It makes it possible for Christians to ignore or even oppose efforts to assist the poor and oppressed, for such efforts may be seen as distractions from central kingdom concerns.

Second, this model may have a too narrow view of the signs of the kingdom. It tends to see evidence of the kingdom's coming only in conversions or in the growth of the church or perhaps in miracles, spiritual gifts, or natural disasters. Typically this model neglects organic and ecological images and understandings found in other models and in Scripture. It tends to see "signs" in the social and political realm not as signs of the kingdom but rather as "signs of the times"—that is, signs of judgment and the coming Apocalypse, which signal the final inbreaking of the kingdom of God.

A third difficulty with this model is that its emphasis on future hope may underplay God's grace or the present work of the Holy Spirit other than in rather individualistic or apocalyptic senses. Generally this model would have difficulty, for example, showing how God's grace might be at work in the arts or in science and technology, with the result that these areas may be seen as irrelevant or even opposed to the work of the kingdom.

Despite its liabilities, this model has at least three abiding values. First, it does have considerable apparent biblical foundation. It takes seriously the extensive biblical material concerning the future, especially that found in Daniel, Ezekiel, Revelation, and the apocalyptic passages in the Gospels. Hermeneutically, however, it tends to find literal meaning in the symbolism of apocalyptic passages while treating figuratively passages that speak of social justice or the poor.

Second, this model strongly maintains the future accent that is a fundamental element of the Christian conception of God's reign. The New Testament and early Christian proclamation of the kingdom—though it centered in the life, death, and resurrection of Jesus Christ—clearly looked forward to the return of Christ and finally to a new heaven and a new earth. This is an essential part of the Christian hope.

We should also observe, finally, that this model has provided and continues to provide hope for Christians in suffering and in difficult circumstances. This element of hope will always give continuing appeal to this understanding of the kingdom—until the kingdom does in fact come in its fullness.

3 MODEL TWO: THE KINGDOM AS INNER SPIRITUAL EXPERIENCE

The kingdom of God is within you. (Luke 17:21)

FOR MANY Christians the kingdom of God is, above all, a reality to be experienced in the heart or soul of the individual believer. To enter the kingdom is to experience God within or to enter into the "beatific vision" of classical Christian spirituality, at least in an anticipatory sense. This is the model of the Interior Kingdom.

In this model the emphasis is not so much on the future as it is on the soul, the inner life of the Christian believer. Teresa of Avila captures the essence of this viewpoint in her mystical writing *The Interior Castle*.[1]

The main characteristics of this model are a strong doctrine of the soul, a stress on salvation as participation in God or "deification," a stress on individual spiritual experience, and the assumption that the "real" world is the realm of the spirit. This understanding of the kingdom may be captured by mystical images of light or fire, or of God's nature as an immense sea. It is reflected in a number of Charles Wesley's hymns, as, for example, in the following:

> Jesus, lover of my soul,
> Let me to thy bosom fly,
> While the nearer waters roll,
> While the tempest still is high.
> Hide me, O my Savior, hide,
> Till the storm of life is past;
> Safe into the haven guide;
> O receive my soul at last.
>
> Plenteous grace with thee is found,
> Grace to cover all my sin;
> Let the healing streams abound,
> Make and keep me pure within.
> Thou of life the fountain art,
> Freely let me take of thee;
> Spring thou up within my heart;
> Rise to all eternity.

A key text for this model is Romans 14:17: "For the kingdom of God is not a matter of eating and drinking, but of righteousness, peace and joy in the Holy Spirit." Since "flesh and blood cannot inherit the kingdom of God" (I Cor. 15:50), clearly the kingdom is essentially a spiritual, nonmaterial reality. Many other Scripture passages express the emphases of this model. Second Peter 1:4 says that Christians "participate in the divine nature." The goal of faith is "the salvation of your souls" (I Pet. 1:9). The mystery of the gospel is "Christ in you, the hope of glory" (Col. 1:27). The Christian's body is "a temple of the Holy Spirit, who is in you, whom you have received from God" (I Cor. 6:19; note also Eph. 3:17-19; Heb. 6:19-20; I John 3:2). The classical text for this model would be, "The kingdom of God is within you" (Luke 17:21).

In this model God reigns above all in the realm of the spirit, which is eternal and unchanging, in contrast to this present material world, which is passing away. To see and experience the kingdom requires spiritual sight, for the kingdom is not visible in society. Fully entering into the kingdom is an ineffable experience that can't really be shared with another human being. The divine being is God the Spirit, who is unseen but with whom the Christian may have deep inner communion. Often, in fact, the relationship with God is understood in such mystical terms that *communion* is not the appropriate word to use. The more fitting word is *union,* and an appropriate image would be that of being lost or immersed in the sea of God's being. To fully experience the kingdom is to be lost in God.

Both this model and the next one, the kingdom as Mystical Communion, focus on the interior life of the believer. The key difference between the two concerns how that inner experience is understood and the degree to which it is shared in Christian community. In the Interior Kingdom model, union with God is such a profound experience that it can't really be communicated to others. Thus this model is the most individualistic of the eight we will be considering.

Given this understanding of Christian experience, one must not expect to discover signs of the kingdom in the world of the senses. The true sign is an inner consciousness of or participation in God. The kingdom is opposed by satanic forces one encounters in one's spiritual pilgrimage, whether in the form of the demonic beings that appeared to Anthony in the desert or in the form of the "dark night of the soul." In more recent psychological interpretations of this tradition these forces may be understood in terms of archetypes or other psychic images or phenomena.

In this model, the true participants in the kingdom are those Christians who go on to perfection in their inner experience of God. The final goal of the kingdom is the absorption of all things into God. As this language implies, "kingdom" or "reign" are less adequate images than more mystical ones which suggest not differentiation from but union with God.

THE MODEL IN HISTORY

In the history of the church, this model may be associated with the early rise of Monasticism in the East and especially with the Desert Fathers, such as Anthony (c. 251–356) and Macarius the Egyptian (c. 300–390). It is grounded, of course, in the New Testament teachings about the believer's inner experience of God through Jesus Christ in conversion and sanctification. As a distinct model it may be traced to the influence of Platonist and Neoplatonist ideas on Christian thinking and especially to Origen. Origen (c. A.D. 185–254) rejected millenarian interpretations of the kingdom altogether and concluded (in Pelikan's words) "that not the body but the soul was the subject of [the biblical] promises, and that therefore the promised kingdom was a purely spiritual one."[2] Clearly this was a profound shift in understanding the kingdom.

Origen was born in Alexandria of Christian parents. His father was martyred when Origen was about sixteen. He became known for his spirituality and for his learning. Most of his voluminous writings sought to make the biblical gospel intelligible in terms of Greek philosophical thought. A pagan contemporary wrote, "While his manner of life was Christian and contrary to the law, he played the Greek, and introduced Greek ideas into foreign fables."[3] Origen himself said, "I want to be a man of the church . . . to be called by the name . . . of Christ, and to bear that name which is blessed on the earth."[4] In the judgment of Robert J. Daly, Origen "has exerted an influence on Christian thought, exceeded perhaps by no one except the apostle Paul himself."[5]

Origen defined the kingdom of God as Jesus Christ and the believer's experience of Christ. Christ, he wrote,

is the King of the heavens, and as He is absolute Wisdom and absolute Righteousness and absolute Truth, is He not so also absolute Kingdom? But it is not a kingdom of any of those below, nor of a part of those above, but of all the things above, which were called heavens. But if you enquire into the meaning of the words, "Theirs is the kingdom of heaven," you may say that Christ is theirs in so far as He is absolute Kingdom, reigning in every thought of the man who is no longer under the reign of sin which reigns in the mortal body of those who have subjected themselves to it. And if I say, reigning in every thought, I mean something like this, reigning as Righteousness and Wisdom and Truth and the rest of the virtues in him who has become a heaven, because of bearing the image of the heavenly, and in every power, whether angelic, or the rest that are named saints, not only in this age, but also in that which is to come, and who are worthy of a kingdom of such a kind.[6]

Christians, "who even now in the present life have been placed in the church, in which we see an imitation of the future kingdom," are to strive for unity and perfection in anticipation of the final restoration. For "the order of our human race was constituted in the hope of restoring it in the age to come, or in the ages beyond that, when there shall be the 'new heaven and new earth,'" to perfect unity.[7]

"The end of the world and the consummation," wrote Origen, "will come when every soul shall be visited with the penalties due for its sins. This time, when everyone shall pay what he owes, is known to God alone. We believe, however, that the goodness of God through Christ will restore his entire creation to one end, even his enemies being conquered and subdued."[8] "Subjection to Christ," as the Apostle Paul uses the phrase in I Corinthians 15, implies not just subordination but salvation. Origen believed that as "the end is always like the beginning" so everything will be "restored, through God's goodness, through their subjection to Christ and their unity with the Holy Spirit, to one end, which is like the beginning."[9]

Origen's speculations (as he regarded them) about the endtimes were really secondary to his emphasis on the Christian's present experience of Christ in the soul. Stressing the spirit over the flesh, Origen said the believer's resurrection would be spiritual, not physical. In Jesus "there began the union of the divine with the human nature, in order that the human, by communion with the divine, might rise to be divine, not in Jesus alone, but in all those who not only believe, but enter upon the life which Jesus taught, and which elevates to friendship with God and communion with Him every one who lives according to the precepts of Jesus."[10]

Origen's views, mediated through Gregory of Nyssa (c. 332–395) and the other Cappadocian Fathers, became an important part of the theological foundation for the monastic movement. Arising in Syria, Egypt, and elsewhere in the East in the third and fourth centuries, monasticism soon spread to the Western church. Particularly influential was Anthony of Egypt, both because of his long life of ascetic piety and because of Athanasius's widely popular *Life of St. Anthony* (c. A.D. 357), which vividly pictured Anthony's battle with demons in the desert.

As a young man Anthony heard in church the Scripture, "If you want to be perfect, go, sell your possessions and give to the poor, and you will have treasure in heaven" (Matt. 19:21). Anthony obeyed literally. Eventually he moved into the desert, where he lived the rest of his life, partly as a hermit and partly as a spiritual director for others who sought him out. According to Athanasius, Anthony "used to say that we ought to devote all our time to the soul instead of the body. . . . For this is what was said by the Savior: 'Do not be anxious for your life, what you shall eat, nor about your body, what you shall put on. . . . Instead, seek his Kingdom, and these things shall be yours as well.' "[11] "Now the Greeks leave home and traverse the sea in order to gain an education," says Athanasius, "but there is no need for us to go abroad on account of the Kingdom of heaven, or to cross the sea for virtue. For the Lord has told us before, 'the Kingdom of God is within you.' "[12]

Athanasius's *Life of St. Anthony* later (in its Latin translation) influenced Augustine and others in the Western church. The book is a seminal work of spirituality that may be thought of as a paradigm of the Interior Kingdom.

Growing from these roots, the mystical tradition in both the East and the West perpetuated a rich and diverse spirituality that continues to the present. Often this tradition has little to say about the kingdom of God because its focus and controlling images are found elsewhere. When it does speak of the kingdom, however, it pictures it in highly interior, spiritualized ways. In fact we may conceive of this tradition as transmuting the biblical teachings on the kingdom into a tradition of primarily interior spirituality. In its focus on the inner experience of the individual believer, monasticism illustrates the Interior Kingdom model. To the degree that it developed a strong communal sense, however, the monastic tradition better illustrates model three, the kingdom as Mystical Communion, to be discussed in the next chapter.

A number of Christian mystics exemplify the Interior Kingdom model. These include John Climacus (c. A.D. 579–649) and Julian of Norwich (c. 1343–1416) among others. In the mystical tradition the kingdom of God in fact rarely even appears as a specific theme, for the focus is on the immediate mystical experience of God. Practically speaking, there is little other real meaning to God's kingdom.

A good illustration is the sixteenth-century Spanish mystic Teresa of Avila (1515–1582), who figured prominently in the Catholic Reformation. In her masterpiece *The Interior Castle,* Teresa describes the soul as "a castle made entirely out of a diamond or of very clear crystal, in which there are many rooms, just as in heaven there are many dwelling places," and in which at the center "is the room or royal chamber where the King stays."[13] Earlier in *The Way of Perfection* she had written, "Let us imagine that within us is an extremely rich palace, built entirely of gold and precious stones; in sum, built for a Lord such as this. . . . Imagine, also, that in this palace dwells this mighty King."[14] As summarized by an early biographer of Teresa, "In the center, the King of Glory dwelt in the greatest splendor. From there He beautified and illumined all those dwelling places to the outer wall. The inhabitants received more light the nearer they were to the center."[15]

The interior castle is a striking picture of God in Christ reigning in the human soul. Teresa writes to encourage and instruct her sister Carmelite nuns who may find their monasteries crowded or confining and who are under the authority of the prioress, yet who may at will "without permission from the prioress . . . enter [the interior castle] and take a walk through it at any time." She adds, "Once you get used to enjoying this castle, you will find rest in all things, even those involving much labor, for you will have the hope of returning to the castle, which no one can take from you."[16] In this imagery Christ is not only King, but he is also Friend, Companion, and Spouse.

Here the Interior Kingdom is clearly pictured. As Teresa understood it, however, God's reign in the soul did not mean that the kingdom had no larger or this-worldly dimensions, for God is sovereign over all. Teresa writes, "The King is in His palace and there are many wars in his kingdom and many painful things going on, but not on that account does he fail to be at his post. So here, even though in those other dwelling places there is much tumult and there are many poisonous creatures and the noise is heard, no one enters that center dwelling place and makes the soul leave."[17] Teresa herself was active in the world and, together with John of the Cross, helped to reform the Carmelite Order. Yet, the interior experience of God clearly was at the center of her life. "Her combination of mystic experience with ceaseless activity as a reformer and organizer makes her life the classic instance for those who contend that the highest contemplation is not incompatible with great practical achievements."[18]

Christian leaders who represent this tradition and in fact have been nurtured by it include people as diverse as Thomas à Kempis, Meister Eckhart, Johann Arndt, George Fox, John Wesley, and Georgia Harkness. Harkness wrote *The Dark Night of the Soul* in 1945 after a period of crisis and spiritual searching. In the book she spoke of the importance of prayer, service, and other means of grace in finding one's way out of depression into a sense of the reality of God's kingdom.[19] She wrote to a reader who found the book helpful, "I should not have been able to write the book if I had not been through it myself. . . . I trust that you may continue to find richness and strength of spiritual experience."[20] In her book *Understanding the Kingdom of God,* which discusses varying views of the kingdom, Harkness says that to enter the kingdom "is to find through the Holy Spirit wisdom, strength, and guidance for living; comfort in sorrow; hope in adversity; outreach in service to others; and an abiding sense of the forgiving and sustaining presence of God."[21] While the kingdom also has its social and eschatological dimensions, as Harkness noted, she apparently found its central meaning in its interior reality.

In more recent decades this model has emerged in the writings of people like Morton Kelsey and others who have used Jungian psychology and symbolism to interpret and supplement the mystical tradition.[22] George Fox's doctrine of the "inner light" to some degree suggests this model, though he, Wesley, and a number of others who stressed Christian community drew on other models as well.

REFORMATION VIEWS OF THE KINGDOM

Protestantism has often stressed religious experience. Justification by faith to the Reformers was not mere doctrine; it was, at least for many, profound, life-changing experience. Of his own discovery of the meaning of salvation by grace through faith, Martin Luther wrote, "Thereupon I felt myself to be reborn and to have gone through open doors into paradise. The whole of Scripture took on a new meaning, and whereas before the 'justice of God' had filled me with hate, now it became to me inexpressibly sweet in greater love. This passage of Paul [Rom. 1:17] became to me a gate to heaven."[23]

This language of individual inner experience and of "paradise" and "heaven" raises the question of whether the primary model of the kingdom in Protestantism is the Interior Kingdom. All the models of the kingdom we are examining in this book occur in one way or another in Protestantism. Future hope, mystical communion, and the transformation of society, particularly, have at times been strong Protestant notes. I would argue, however, that the dominant, though seldom exclusive, model of the kingdom in Protestantism has been that of the kingdom as inner spiritual experience.

In most of the Reformers this model is fundamental but occurs in less mystical form than the examples we have seen so far. Though one finds in the Reformers other themes as well, notably the kingdom as future hope and a close identification of the kingdom with the invisible church, the Interior Kingdom remains the central model.

Luther expresses this clearly when he speaks of Christ as

> the true and only first-born of God the Father and the Virgin Mary and true king and priest, but not after the fashion of the flesh and the world, for his kingdom is not of this world. He reigns in heavenly and spiritual things and consecrates them—things such as righteousness, truth, wisdom, peace, salvation, etc. This does not mean that all things on earth and in hell are not also subject to him—otherwise how could he protect and save us from them?—but that his kingdom consists neither in them nor of them.[24]

L. Berkhof notes that the Reformers "did not formulate a doctrine of the Kingdom as clear-cut and elaborate as that of the Middle Ages, nor could they point to such a concrete embodiment of the earthly reign of Christ as the Church of Rome. They agreed in identifying it with the invisible Church, the community of the elect, or of the saints of God. For them it was first of all a religious concept, the reign of God in the hearts of believers, the *regnum Christi spirituale* or *internum*," though they did not overlook its ethical import. They recognized the authority of civil government and opposed Radical Protestant attempts "to set up in the world an external Kingdom of God...They did not expect the external visible form of the Kingdom of God until the glorious appearance of Jesus Christ."[25]

Because of their unavoidable involvement with the politics of their time, the "magisterial" Reformers (particularly Luther and Calvin) have often been seen as articulating a rather political conception of God's reign—Luther's "two kingdoms" or Calvin's Genevan "theocracy."* But this is a misunderstanding. The Reformers saw the kingdom as primarily inward and spiritual, but since all things come from God and belong to God, believers must responsibly be involved in all areas of life. Luther's and Calvin's concern with Christian vocation was no secularizing or politicizing of God's kingdom; rather it was precisely *because of* their certainty that God's reign is primarily spiritual that they insisted that governing leaders use their political stewardship to promote God's truth. This is the starting point, the foundation upon which they built their teachings on church, state, and vocation.

Luther saw the kingdom of God and the kingdom of Satan as being in mortal conflict throughout history. "For there is no middle kingdom between the kingdom of God and the kingdom of Satan, which are ever at war with each other."[26] But in the present, God's kingdom, essentially spiritual, remains mysterious and hidden. Luther looked forward to the future kingdom in its fullness when all creation would be reconciled (Rom. 8:20-21) after the present form of the world is destroyed by fire.

In Luther's view, God has instituted the state to restrain evil and prevent chaos. Heinrich Bornkamm summarizes Luther's perspective as follows: "The state is essentially an institution of force and coercion and, therefore, the antithesis of the kingdom of God. . . . Nevertheless, the state is a divine institution. It is not essentially Christian" but is the agency of God's preserving work.[27] This is Luther's theory of the two kingdoms. Luther writes:

> There are two kingdoms, one the kingdom of God, the other the kingdom of the world. . . . God's kingdom is a kingdom of grace and mercy . . . but the kingdom of the world is a kingdom of wrath and severity. . . . Now he who would confuse these two kingdoms—as our false fanatics do—would put wrath into God's kingdom and mercy into the world's kingdom; and that is the same as putting the devil in heaven and God in hell.[28]

Luther was steering here between Roman Catholicism, which in his day identified the kingdom with Rome and the church, and "radicals" who insisted that the kingdom of God had no place for the sword. Schematically his two-kingdoms view may be represented as follows:[29]

Kingdom of the World	Kingdom of God
Under the law	Under the gospel
State	Church
Society, nominal Christians	True believers
Law	Grace
Limits sin	Promotes gospel
Power of sword	Power of Word

In this schema rulers in their official capacity must follow the law, not the gospel, even if they are Christians.

It would seem that Luther's views constitute, more accurately, a theology of three kingdoms: the gracious kingdom of God; the political kingdom of law; and the subversive kingdom of Satan. God reigns eternally over all, but hiddenly, in the kingdom of grace, which will ultimately triumph. Yet, in present history he reigns also through the kingdom of law, which acts to restrain the Satanic kingdom until it is finally destroyed when the gracious kingdom triumphs in glory. There is a certain political realism to this view, and, of course, its practical effect is to justify the use of coercion by the state, even when exercised by Christians. In this whole framework, however, the primary conception is that of an inner, spiritual kingdom.

In *Christ and Culture* H. Richard Niebuhr cites Luther as his primary example of the "Christ and Culture in Paradox" position. While Luther distinguishes the two kingdoms, he insists that Christians are to be fully involved in the world even with all the contradictions this entails. Niebuhr notes: "Luther does not . . . divide what he distinguishes. The life in Christ and the life in culture, in the kingdom of God and the kingdom of the world, are closely related. The Christian must affirm both in a single act of obedience to the one God of mercy and wrath, not as a divided soul with a double allegiance and duty."[30] Luther held this view, says Niebuhr, because "he thoroughly understood that the gospel as law and as promise was not directly concerned with the overt actions of men but with the springs of conduct; that it was the measure by which God recreated the souls of men so that they might really perform good works."[31] This view can easily lead, however, to a kind of practical dualism in which one lives spiritually or inwardly by the kingdom of God but outwardly in a contrary way. This is in fact one of the fundamental problems of the Interior Kingdom model.

We find a similar perspective in John Calvin—not a doctrine of two kingdoms, but certainly a doctrine of an inner spiritual kingdom. Calvin is clear on this when in the *Institutes of the Christian Religion* he discusses the kingly office of Christ (after considering Christ as Prophet and Priest). He writes, "Everything which is earthly, and of the world, is temporary, and soon fades away. Christ, therefore, to raise our hope to the heavens, declares that his kingdom is not of this world (John xviii. 36). In fine, let each of us, when he hears that the kingdom of Christ is spiritual, be roused by the thought to entertain the hope of a better life, and to expect that as it is now protected by the hand of Christ, so it will be fully realized in a future life."[32] The kingdom of Christ, "not being earthly or carnal, and so subject to corruption, but spiritual . . . raises us even to eternal life, so that we can patiently live at present under toil, hunger, cold, contempt, disgrace, and other annoyances; contented with this, that our King will never abandon us, but will supply our necessities until our warfare is ended, and we are called to triumph; such being the nature of his kingdom, that he communicates to us whatever he received of his Father."[33]

Calvin's view of the kingdom was oriented more toward social engagement and life in the world generally than were those of many who represent the Interior Kingdom model. "When our Lord Jesus Christ appeared," Calvin said, "he acquired possession of the whole world; and his kingdom was extended from one end of it to the other, especially with the proclamation of the Gospel. . . . God has consecrated the entire earth through the precious blood of his Son to the end that we may inhabit it and live under his reign." Christians, he said, must "recognize that we remain unworthy to look upon heaven until there is harmony and unanimity in religion, till God is purely worshiped by all, and all the world is reformed."[34] Christians have responsibility for redemptive witness in all areas of life to the end that God's sovereignty may be recognized. Here is the basis for the Christian cultural witness that has been emphasized by many Dutch Calvinists, the Institute for Christian Studies in Toronto, and, in a somewhat different way, Francis Schaeffer.[35] Yet, for Calvin himself (as for Schaeffer) such activity flows from rather than replaces the fundamentally inner and spiritual nature of God's reign.

Calvin's understanding of the relationship between church and state has often been viewed as theocratic: God actually reigning through the political power structures. Whether Calvin really sees God's reign as a theocracy is a question we will need to examine when we discuss our sixth model, the kingdom as political state.

In general we may say that for the Reformers the kingdom of God is most basically a spiritual reality with inner, ethical, and eschatological dimensions. At one level the Reformers were mystics and drew on the mystical tradition; yet, their emphasis, in contrast with the mystical tradition, was more Christ *for* us than Christ *in* us; more on the objective *fact* (as they saw it) of God's spiritual reign than the subjective *experience* of that reign; more on the Word than on the Spirit. It is at this point that the Lutheran Pietism of Johann Arndt, Philip Spener, and August Francke, or the spirituality of George Fox or John Wesley, combines or synthesizes the mystical and the classical Protestant traditions. In all these cases the primary model is the same, but the combination with secondary models leads to quite different results in individual cases.

John Wesley (1703–1791) represents this model in several ways: in his early attraction to the mysticism of William Law and others, in his continuing use of literature from this tradition throughout his life, and in his emphasis on God's providence and spiritual rule. Wesley ultimately rejected mysticism as a primary model for understanding salvation and God's relationship to the world. Throughout his life, however, he showed an affinity for the emphasis on interior spirituality and participation in the divine nature. Wesley's use of Macarius the Egyptian and Ephrem Syrus is an example of this, and his doctrine of entire sanctification is in part indebted to it.

The Interior Kingdom model is implied in much popular Christian piety, especially that growing out of the American Revivalist tradition. It is seen in many popular nineteenth-century hymns and gospel songs, such as Fanny Crosby's "Blessed Assurance" (1873) and in Charles Gabriel's 1902 hymn, "He Is So Precious to Me":

> 'Tis heaven below my Redeemer to know,
> For He is so precious to me.

Many of these songs are written in the first person singular—the perspective of the individual believer. Other examples are books such as Hannah Whitall Smith's *The Christian's Secret of a Happy Life,* first published in 1870 and still in print today, several million copies later. Smith's images of "divine union" and "the life on wings" are pictures of the kingdom as inner spiritual experience.[36] Much of the popular devotional literature of our time also seems to assume such a model; for example, the widely used devotional guides *Our Daily Bread* and *The Upper Room.*

The Interior Kingdom seems to be the primary model also of Carl F. H. Henry in his recent systematic theology. One of Henry's theological theses is: "Divine revelation is given for human benefit, offering us privileged communion with our Creator in the kingdom of God."[37] The kingdom is something believers experience through faith in Christ. Henry insists, however, that the kingdom also has significant historical and cultural dimensions. He writes:

> We are already in the kingdom; we share in eternal life, live on speaking terms with the Lord in whom we have our new life and who indwells us. We are quickened by the power of the Holy Spirit to do his will and enlisted in the historical expansion of the kingdom from heaven to earth. The rule of the King is therefore far more than just a hope of redeemed individuals. We must not

ignore the present claims that the rule of God makes upon government and society, nor must we minimize the fact that God is everywhere present and active either in grace or in judgment, even if in modern times the worldwide mission of the church has often become confused with a social and political idealism that reduces the kingdom of God to extending democracy or free enterprise or socialism or brotherhood among unregenerate humanity and substitutes a present activist-promoted millennium for one inaugurated by the Messiah.[38]

Although the kingdom is "not of this world," Henry says, it exists "not on some invisible and inaccessible planet"; it is in some ways "already a historical reality even here on earth where the risen Lord is sovereign in a kingdom that exists alongside other kingdoms and interpenetrates and confronts them as an invincible reality." All of human life and activity is under God's judgment. "The church even at her best is but an approximation of the kingdom of God, [thus] only the grace of Christ can avail for any of us. For all that, the kingdom is nonetheless not without historical presence and power."[39] It is a kingdom of righteousness and justice "because justice has its very foundation and essential structure in the kingdom of God."[40]

Henry has called for "evangelical demonstration" of the gospel in society, based on the central Christian conviction of "the lordship of Christ as the ruler of nature, the sovereign of the nations and the decisive center of history." Yet, Christians must be clear about "the Biblical insistence on internal spiritual transformation of man's sinful nature as a prerequisite for the Kingdom of God both here and hereafter."[41]

Thus Henry views the kingdom as *more than* an inner or future spiritual reality. But it is essentially a spiritual reality experienced inwardly and in the church's communion with God. His primary models, then (though not his only ones), would seem to be models two and three. His strong emphasis on doctrine and presuppositional truth places him closer to Calvin than to Teresa of Avila, as one would expect; closer to classical Protestant orthodoxy than to mystical visions of the Interior Kingdom.

In his book *Kingdoms in Conflict,* Charles Colson sets forth a view much like Henry's, particularly stressing Christian responsibility in society. He criticizes the tendency to view the kingdom as too otherworldy, even though its fundamental nature is spiritual. "Through the centuries," argues Colson, many Christians "have watered down [Jesus'] teaching, stripped away His demands for the building of a righteous society, and preached an insipid religion concerned only with personal benefits. This distorted view portrays Christianity not as the powerful source of spiritual rebirth and the mediating force for justice, mercy, and love in the world, but as the ultimate self-fulfillment plan."[42]

In Colson's view, the kingdom is both present and future, though in its present form it is primarily unseen and spiritual. "The Kingdom of God embraces every aspect of life: ethical, spiritual, and temporal," he writes. But it "is not a blueprint for some new social order; nor does it merely set the forces of radical cultural change in motion. Rather, God's Kingdom promises radical changes in human personalities." He adds, "While human politics is based on the premise that society must be changed in order to change people, in the politics of the Kingdom it is people who must be changed in order to change society."[43]

Colson represents the views of many Christians whose primary model is the Interior Kingdom but who insist that the gospel calls us to work for righteousness and justice in society. He cites William Wilberforce's successful efforts in England to outlaw the slave trade as a primary example. This is not the Transforming Kingdom model (model seven in our typology), for the primary focus is personal evangelism, not social transformation. But social witness is seen as the normal and necessary responsibility of kingdom Christians.

ASSESSING THE MODEL

As our discussion has shown, the Interior Kingdom model draws to some degree on Greek philosophical roots. One can often sense the Platonism lying behind this model, however this may be modified by biblical categories and themes.

This model does not deny that God does or will ultimately reign visibly on earth, but it sees that fact as largely irrelevant to present Christian experience and the life of the church because Christ already reigns in the heart. The primary function of the church is to provide access to the spiritual kingdom. In most versions of this model, "kingdom" or "reign" as a metaphor has less force than do more mystical or relational images, such as love and marriage, identification with Christ's passion, or perhaps God as Mother (rather than Monarch).[44]

This does not mean, however, that feminists or others who wish to use feminine or maternal images of God necessarily would feel comfortable with the interior model of the kingdom. Contemporary feminist critiques of monarchical images of God seem to imply the rejection of the model of kingdom altogether. To the degree that feminist conceptions of God and salvation correspond to the typology being used here, they generally fit more nearly our eighth model, the kingdom as earthly utopia, understood particularly in an ecological sense.[45]

Several positive values of this model should be noted. First, it gives intimate, personal meaning to the kingdom. It connects with the deep human hunger and thirst to know God. This vision of the kingdom, therefore, has a power and immediacy that often have made it appealing down through the centuries and still make it attractive today for many Christians.

The inward kingdom is often a source of comfort and strength for people who are suffering or oppressed. "Pie in the sky when you die" understandings of Christianity have often been ridiculed for making people passive in the face of injustice. Still, this conception of the kingdom frequently has enabled Christians to live with hope and compassion through times of persecution, illness, or poverty, giving them a sense of God and of spiritual reality that has been experienced as more real and powerful than one's outward circumstances.

A second strength of the Interior Kingdom model is that it can claim considerable biblical support, especially from New Testament writers. Whereas the Future Kingdom model appeals to prophetic and apocalyptic passages, this model points to Scriptures that speak of the indwelling Christ, the fullness of the Holy Spirit, and inward communion with God. It uses such passages to interpret the meaning of others that speak more specifically about the kingdom.

It may be viewed as a strength of this model, third, that it accents the spiritual nature of God's kingdom. This is a counterweight to secularizing tendencies or to conceptions of the kingdom that make God's reign too this-worldly, sacrificing its transcendent dimensions. Whatever the weaknesses of this model, it maintains a strong God-consciousness: God not as impersonal force or absentee sovereign, but God of personal moral character who desires communion with men and women and who, through the work of Jesus Christ and the presence of the Spirit, makes this possible.[46]

Down through the centuries, Christians of the Interior Kingdom tradition have demonstrated the reality of God and the possibility of a deep inner correspondence between God's Spirit and our spirit. Human beings, to use a favorite phrase of John and Charles Wesley, are "capable of God." The inward kingdom model underscores this fundamental human capability, enabled by grace, to experience God.

The emphasis on "capability" can, of course, potentially lead to a theological problem. It is not always clear in this model what the role of Jesus Christ is or in what sense he is necessary in order that one may experience God. In fact, in some cases this model of the kingdom departs from historic Christian orthodoxy into varieties of mysticism that can hardly be described as fully Christian. One may cite here those mystics down through the history of the church who often existed on the fringes of Christian orthodoxy, many of whom were eventually judged to be heretical. Today we may raise similar questions about the often unclear boundaries between New Age thinking and some forms of Christian spirituality based on a sort of panreligious syncretism, or perhaps a pantheistic spirituality that is not distinctly Christian. In the main, however, the interior model has focused on Jesus Christ (or, at times, on Mary), though generally in a highly individualistic way.

We may point, finally, to several limitations of the Interior Kingdom model. Most important, it tends to undervalue the believer's present life on earth and in society. It is in this sense world-denying, seeing little value in the material world, including politics and economics. Or, with Luther, the model may place the material and the spiritual worlds quite literally in different realms.

Historically this model has often been tainted with a sort of Platonic disdain for things material, perhaps seeing the body or matter as evil or at least imperfect and imperfectible. It is thus dualistic, viewing the "higher" spiritual world as essentially separate from the material world. One can participate in the kingdom only in a spiritual sense. It is true, nevertheless, that historically many Christians who represent this model were actively engaged in the affairs of their day (Luther and Teresa of Avila, for example).

A second liability of the Interior Kingdom model is its heavy individualism. Granted, this individualism is in a sense transcended as the Christian's being and identity are in some measure lost in God ("participation in the divine nature"), or as Christians join together monastically or in congregations in their quest for God. Yet, the kingdom is really not a socially shared reality in any practical sense. Many of the heroes of this model were for the most part solitary figures who found God and participated in the heavenly kingdom pretty much in isolation from other Christians. There is, of course, an obvious link between this fact and the previously mentioned dualism and undervaluing of this-worldly existence.

Contemporary instances of this model may not necessarily view the material or social world negatively—in some cases, quite the opposite! A dualistic mind-set that radically separates things spiritual from things material may in fact be more hedonistic than ascetic. One thinks of the so-called prosperity gospel: "All this and heaven too!" Here the Interior Kingdom model is curiously joined to the Earthly Utopia model, as we shall see in chapter 8. On the one hand, the kingdom is totally spiritual and future. On the other hand, since Christians know they are accepted by God and are already granted citizenship in the heavenly kingdom, they can and should expect to enjoy material "blessings" now as a sign, or at least as a reasonable benefit, of God's grace. The individualism of such a conception of God's kingdom is evident. Christians who hold this view tend to see present "blessings" of the kingdom in rather personal, private, and self-centered terms. In the United States, this fits well with the ruggedly individualistic, private enterprise mind-set that has characterized much conservative Protestantism.

Biblically speaking, this model negates much of the Old Testament by over-spiritualizing its prophetic vision. Very earthly, this-worldly prophecies of God's coming kingdom are taken to symbolize the blessings of heaven or of the soul's communion with God. Or they are treated as types of the coming of Christ and of salvation through him. This approach cuts the nerve of the ethical and social thrust of much biblical prophecy. The Old Testament is not sufficiently taken on its own terms but is too radically reinterpreted in the light of the New Testament.[47]

As already noted, this is the most individualistic model of the kingdom— a significant point of criticism. When John Wesley said that he nearly shipwrecked his faith on mysticism, he was referring to this individualistic element. He discovered in his quest for Christian perfection that if he were really to be holy he must search for holiness not in isolation but in the company of others. This is what Wesley meant by "social holiness." While the kingdom of God certainly is an inner reality, it is not exclusively that. Individualistic conceptions of the kingdom can undercut the transforming power of the kingdom both in the church and in society.

Relatedly, this model of the kingdom in most of its forms is overly other-worldly and escapist. Even more than model one, it holds out little hope for the present order. Christians may do good works and show genuine compassion as an expression of their experience of God, but they do so with little sense of cooperating with or contributing toward a new order that God is bringing about on earth. This earth ultimately is but a shadow. It is passing away, for the true kingdom of God is of the spirit.

4 MODEL THREE: THE KINGDOM AS MYSTICAL COMMUNION

I confer on you a kingdom . . . so that you may eat and drink
at my table in my kingdom. (Luke 22:29-30)

THE KINGDOM of God may be understood as inner spiritual experience but in a less individualistic, more social sense—the kingdom as "mystical communion." This is a distinct model with its own history in the Christian tradition. We may call it the model of the Heavenly Kingdom.

In this conception the kingdom of God is closely associated with the idea of the "communion of saints" as this came to be understood historically as "communion between the heavenly and the earthly Church and its members,"[1] and so primarily in a mystical sense. This conception is less individualistic than the first model, for the kingdom involves the spiritual communion of all believers—those on earth now and those who have gone before. The kingdom is an invisible corporate reality, not bound by space and time, which we experience now in anticipation of a fuller reality to come.

"The communion of saints" has, of course, often been understood as a description of the church.[2] The church is mystically the community of saints on earth and saints in heaven, a vital spiritual connection all along the whole line of Christians constantly in holy procession from earth to glory as history moves forward. So are we really talking here about the church or about the kingdom?

In a sense, both. From the standpoint of the earthly experience of Christians, the communion of saints refers primarily to the church. But viewed, as it were, from above and from the future, the communion of saints appropriately signifies the kingdom of God. For clarity, however, we will speak of the communion of saints primarily as the church which now spiritually partakes proleptically of the kingdom, and refer to this model of God's reign as the mystical or heavenly kingdom.

This model can draw on many of the Scriptures mentioned in the previous chapter and on passages like Ephesians 2:21-22, which speaks of Christians as "a holy temple," "a dwelling in which God lives by his Spirit." Often the paradigm of this view, however, is the disciples' experience on the Mount of Transfiguration, particularly as recorded by Luke. In Luke 9:26-27 Jesus speaks of the Son of Man returning "in his glory and in the glory of the Father," adding that some who were then present would "not taste death before they see the kingdom of God." Luke's account then proceeds directly to the Transfiguration (9:28-36), in which some of those present in the previous passage (Peter, James, and John) "saw his glory" (9:32). It is not difficult to conclude here that "seeing the kingdom of God" and seeing Christ's glory are the same thing. Thus to share in such a mystical experience with Christ and other saints (those who have gone before— e.g., Moses and Elijah; those of the present-day—the disciples) is to experience now the kingdom of God. As Peter, James, and John saw the glory of God on the mountain, away from everyday life, when Christ was transfigured before them, so we experience the kingdom of God when we enter into spiritual communion with Christ and all the saints. The experience of these disciples with Jesus on the Mount becomes a root image for this understanding of the kingdom. (This interpretation does in fact provide an answer to the difficult question of what Jesus meant when he said, "Some who are standing here will not taste death before they see the kingdom of God.")

The Last Supper, with its hints of eschatological fulfillment, and the picture of the "great multitude" in Revelation 7:9-17 can also be cited in support of the mystical communion model. Both speak of a people gathered in the worship of God, and together they suggest the church both as a "little flock" and as a "great multitude" united in spiritual communion and doxological purpose.

Jesus' last supper with his disciples was both a culmination of his earthly ministry with those he had chosen (John 15:16) and an anticipation of the expected kingdom of God which the disciples were still expecting. In Luke 22:25-30 Jesus speaks of kingdoms and servanthood and then concludes: "You are those who have stood by me in my trials. And I confer on you a kingdom, just as my Father conferred one on me, so that you may eat and drink at my table in my kingdom and sit on thrones, judging the twelve tribes of Israel" (Luke 22:28-29). Both Matthew and Mark report that on serving the wine Jesus said, "I will not drink again of the fruit of the vine until that day when I drink it anew in the kingdom of God" (Mark 14:25). Matthew has, significantly, "drink it anew *with you* in my Father's kingdom" (Matt. 26:29, italics added). The parallel passages in John do not specifically mention the kingdom but, with their stress on the Spirit and on leaving and returning, clearly have eschatological overtones.

A number of passages in Revelation may be seen as the fulfillment (at least in part) of Jesus' words to his disciples about the kingdom. Christ "has made us to be a kingdom and priests to serve his God and Father" (Rev. 1:6). Jesus will come and live with all who open the door to him (Rev. 3:20). The climax is the vision of the "great multitude that no one could count, from every nation, tribe, people and language, standing before the throne and in front of the Lamb" (Rev. 7:9), who cry out:

> Salvation belongs to our God,
> who sits on the throne,
> and to the Lamb. (Rev. 7:10)

MARKS OF THE MODEL

This is the model, then, in which the kingdom is especially linked to the communion of saints. It is not so much the individual soul as the Christian community in which God dwells. In worship Christians enter into communion through the Spirit with God and other believers—those physically present and the whole company of the saints who have gone before. In worship, time and space are transcended as one glorifies God "with all the saints."

The focus on worship and liturgy thus distinguishes this model from the Interior Kingdom. It is especially in worship that one experiences the communion of the saints. Here believers enter into fellowship with the heavenly realm under God's sovereign rule. As in the first model, the accent is on the heavenly, not the earthly.

With its focus on worship, this model tends also to be highly sacramental—either in the traditional sense of the Christian sacraments or in the more general sense that worship both symbolizes and actualizes the mystery of communion with God and with and in the mystical body of Christ.

In this model, the kingdom now is a foretaste of heaven. In fact, the kingdom and heaven become virtually synonymous. Little distinction is made between the two, so that to enter heaven is to enter the kingdom of God. The kingdom's ultimate reality is in the next world, beyond this life. But we may participate now in that eternal realm through the communion of saints. In popular spirituality "heaven" and "kingdom" may be used interchangeably, for heaven becomes a fundamental symbol of the kingdom. This is the Kingdom of Heaven, the heavenly kingdom. A number of hymns and gospel songs illustrate this, such as "On Jordan's Stormy Banks I Stand," "Glorious Things of Thee Are Spoken," and Fanny Crosby's hymn "Some Day the Silver Cord Will Break":

> Some day the silver cord will break,
> And I no more as now shall sing;
> But oh, the joy when I shall wake
> Within the palace of the King!

Within this model, the church may be described as the communion of saints (as we have noted) and as the sacrament of the kingdom. Avery Dulles suggests in his discussion of the church and eschatology:

> Throughout the Patristic period, Christian preachers and theologians looked upon the Church as the communion of saints that exists imperfectly here on earth and perfectly in the blessed in heaven. Heaven exists not only in the future but even now in the saints who have gone before us. . . .
>
> Medieval monasticism was concerned to achieve on earth the most perfect replica of heaven that could be attained. For Bernard of Clairvaux the monk should live here on earth the life of the blessed, undistracted by the demands of the body and all worldly concerns. To some extent this may have been an evasion of worldly responsibilities, but it was an attractive ideal that in many ways proved beneficial to culture. The high spiritual ideals of monastic theology permeated the art, architecture, literature, and music of the Middle Ages.[3]

Dulles notes also the sacramental language of the document *Lumen gentium* of Vatican II. Here "the Church is the Kingdom of heaven now present in mystery." The church "is seen as eschatological insofar as it is a sacrament of the eschatological Kingdom."[4] Both these images—communion of saints and sacrament—seem to express the model of the kingdom as mystical communion, though for Dulles these represent two different models of the church, the one mystical and the other sacramental. Both church models may reflect similar conceptions of the kingdom.

The sacramental understanding of the church also connects strongly with the kingdom as institutional church, which we will discuss in the next chapter. In fact, an interesting observation may be made here. For centuries (in Roman Catholicism especially, but also to a lesser degree in Eastern Orthodoxy and Protestantism) the "mystical communion" and institutional-sacramental conceptions of the church and the kingdom have existed simultaneously and interdependently. One value of a sacramental understanding of the church (as Dulles also notes) is that with its aspects of sign and mystery it is capable of holding together emphases that seem in tension. This is the case here. It is the sacramental sense, with its combining of visible signs and invisible mysteries, that holds together two rather different kingdom models: the heavenly or mystical and the institutional. As long as the mystical understanding of the kingdom is tied to or affirms the church's sacramentalism, and as long as the institutional church does not lose a sense of spiritual mystery that is experienced as genuine, these two models of church and kingdom can co-exist. The Reformation may be understood in part as the breakdown of this tension as the church's sacramentalism lost its credibility through the spread of indulgences and other abuses.

In this model of the mystical kingdom, the primary agent is God the Spirit working through the sacraments and the other means of grace, especially prayer. One does not look for signs of the kingdom except as the worshiping, praying community visibly models the kingdom of heaven. The real evidence of the kingdom is the mystery of God's presence in worship and sacrament, which Christians share among themselves in the congregation or in smaller subcommunities (the monastery, the small group, or other *ecclesiolae*). God's kingdom is opposed by "the world, the flesh, and the devil," which are obstacles on the path to heaven. The material world, including the passions of the flesh, are negative forces to be overcome by spiritual discipline and the encouragement that comes from participation in the heavenly community.

The participants in the kingdom are, of course, Christians, but particularly those who follow the counsels of perfection and overcome the temptations of the world. The final goal and culmination of the kingdom is the everlasting worship of God in heaven. For this reason the best biblical picture of the kingdom, according to this model, is John's vision of the great multitude around the heavenly throne (Rev. 4–7) and the Old Testament passages that lie behind it.

In this view the kingdom's present relevance is that it keeps before us the ideal of truth and rectitude as a pattern for our lives so that we will finally gain heaven. The kingdom is viewed as primarily otherworldly and future. As we shall see, however, some forms of this model may be linked with certain dispensational millennial views.

THE MODEL IN HISTORY

This model has been prominent especially in Eastern Orthodox spirituality.[5] It is a dominant model in much Christian mysticism, both in the East and in the West. Good examples would be John of Damascus (c. 675–749) in the East and John Tauler (c. 1300–1361) in the West. In Western Christianity this understanding of God and salvation has had a long influence, especially in sacramental mystical spirituality. The influence of these views can be traced in Lutheranism and particularly in Lutheran Pietism, as well as in Wesley's understanding of Christian perfection.

This conception of the kingdom is also found in much Puritan spirituality. An example is Richard Baxter's *The Saints' Everlasting Rest* (1650). Serious Christians pray that God's kingdom may come, says Baxter; they look ahead to that "Jerusalem which is above" while living a life of contemplation and devotion here. So Baxter writes: "I hope you will value this heavenly life, and take one walk every day in the New Jerusalem."[6] John Milton's *Paradise Lost* (1667) and John Bunyan's *Pilgrim's Progress*

(1678) also had the effect of reinforcing the view of heaven as the essential meaning of the kingdom of God.

The Heavenly Kingdom model has some affinities with John Wesley's views. Wesley's understanding of Christian holiness was both social and sacramental, and this shaped his understanding of the kingdom of God within his overall theology of the economy of salvation.

One would expect Wesley's conception of the kingdom to be rather eclectic and inclusive of several models, since he was decidedly a both/and rather than an either/or thinker. And this is in fact the case. His conception of the kingdom may be viewed as a composite of several models. The kingdom is a deep inner experience of God (model two), as we have seen, but it is also social and sacramental ("mystical communion") with a strong future hope (model one). It is also present and outward, however, leavening society (model seven and, to a lesser degree, model five, "countersystem"). Probably Wesley's view is least like model four, which closely identifies the kingdom with the institutional church.

For Wesley the kingdom of God is synonymous with "true religion." Frequently it is pictured simply as "righteousness, peace and joy in the Holy Spirit" (Rom. 14:17). This is the verse Wesley usually cited in referring to the kingdom of God; he did not often refer to passages that speak of other dimensions of the kingdom. This is because Wesley linked the kingdom to his understanding of sanctification. Fundamentally the kingdom is the direct experience of God through Jesus Christ. Wesley was quick to stress the present implications of the gospel and the requirement of the obedience of good works. But underlying this seems to be an assumption that the real significance of good works and of the present life is their function in preparing us for eternity. Wesley's immersion in the early Greek and medieval Christian tradition is reflected in his view of sanctification. Here the kingdom is understood more as spiritual communion with God and other believers than as a new order within society.

In his stress on both inward and outward holiness, however, Wesley did suggest a present social meaning of the kingdom. By grace, Christians are co-laborers with God in the work of redemption. Wesley saw the present order as an active battle between the kingdom of darkness and the kingdom of God. Christians are not saved *out of* this battle but rather are called *into* it to wrestle with principalities and powers. The Christian life is lived in the light of eternity actively, not passively.

In this sense, the hundreds of little Methodist societies Wesley formed might almost be called "eschatological communities." Only one condition was required to join: a desire "to flee from the wrath to come, to be saved from their sins." There was no doctrinal test, for Wesley was convinced that a person "may be orthodox in every point" and yet "have no religion at all."[7]

Yet, individuals could continue as Methodists only if they submitted to Methodist disciplines and lived lives of faith and good works. The church, said Wesley, is a "body of men compacted together in order, first, to save each his own soul, then to assist each other in working out their salvation, and afterwards, as far as in them lies, to save all men from present and future misery, to overturn the kingdom of Satan, and set up the kingdom of Christ. And this ought to be the continued care and endeavour of every member of his church. Otherwise he is not worthy to be called a member thereof, as he is not a living member of Christ."[8]

In his several sermons on the Sermon on the Mount, Wesley sought to elaborate the way to the kingdom. He wrote: "The Son of God, who came from heaven, is here showing us the way to heaven, to the place which he hath prepared for us, the glory he had before the world began. He is teaching us the true way to life everlasting, the royal way which leads to the kingdom."[9] The "kingdom of heaven" is an "inward kingdom"; it is "heaven already opened in the soul, the first springing up of those rivers of pleasure which flow at God's right hand for evermore."[10] Christ's "little flock" should not fear, for it is God's "good pleasure yet to renew the face of the earth." Eventually "all the kingdoms of the world shall become the kingdoms of our God. . . . They shall all be without spot or blemish, loving one another, even as Christ hath loved us. Be thou part of the first-fruits, if the harvest is not yet. Do thou love thy neighbour as thyself. . . . May thy soul continually overflow with love, swallowing up every unkind and unholy temper, till he calleth thee up into the region of love, there to reign with him for ever and ever!"[11]

Wesley was not much concerned about eschatological road-mapping the extent that he dealt with endtime events he largely took over the views of Bengel and others. His view of Christ's Second Coming was postmillennial, but he did not emphasize the point. His primary focus was much more on the present operation of God's grace and love in believers in the light of the certainty of final judgment and of the "new heaven and new earth" that were sure to come. Human beings, created in God's image, are able through Christ to enjoy now the central meaning of God's kingdom even as they anticipate the kingdom of glory in its final fullness.

Understandably, the Heavenly Kingdom model is found in much revivalistic and Evangelical spirituality of the nineteenth and twentieth centuries in the United States and Great Britain. The call to conversion or to the "higher" or "deeper" life was an invitation to begin enjoying heaven here below. This is reflected in many hymns and gospel songs in this tradition, from "When We All Get to Heaven" to "We're Marching to Zion."

Thomas Oden represents a reaffirmation of the Heavenly Kingdom model in the present day. His new systematic theology, which is based largely on Scripture and a return to classical Christian sources, pictures the kingdom primarily as the communion of saints. God's reign is a kingdom of power, grace, and glory: "The kingdom of power exists amid the dying world in which hiddenly Christ reigns amid and beyond the death of human cultures and artifacts. The church is the kingdom of grace in history, and glory beyond history."[12] "Christ's governance extends to the church in particular and to the world in general, which are preserved through grace until the final days. Within history Christ's kingdom is in but not of the world, hidden in a world sustained by divine providence. Christ's kingly rule is manifested among those who have union with him, the church, which in history includes both wheat and tares (Matt. 13:25-40). The kingdom is already begun, yet awaiting its consummation; in time, yet eternal."[13]

Whereas the kingdom of glory is "that future fulfillment of the messianic mission through which the wrongs of history will be righted," the kingdom of grace is the church's present communion with God. Oden writes:

> The subjects of the dominion of grace are believers united to Christ through word and sacrament. The dominion of grace is the church, which Christ enables, furnishes, equips with gifts requisite to mission, and defends against ever-incipient temptation and apostasy. . . .
>
> The arena in which this kingdom is present is the inner life. It is not a physical or economic sphere subject to empirical identification or material measurement. . . .
>
> The kingdom of grace is governed by preaching the gospel, teaching the covenant community the truth, continuing the restraint of sin by law, providing what is necessary for salvation, pardoning the penitent, justifying by grace, converting through repentance and faith, and sanctifying through the Spirit.
>
> The kingdom of grace is at the same time a kingdom of heaven (because Christ intercedes in heaven) and a kingdom already expectantly received here on earth (because Christ enables citizens of this kingdom to enjoy the fruits of his guidance and protection already in present history).[14]

Thus in Oden's view the kingdom is closely associated with the church as a spiritual communion existing in but transcending time, space, and history. Christ's "rulership" is "preexistent from all eternity" and is "spiritual, not political. He came to establish a spiritual kingdom or governance."[15]

THE KINGDOM AS HEAVEN

As we have seen, in the mystical communion model, heaven and the kingdom of God are often linked as synonyms, especially in popular usage. Through grace Christians now experience "heaven on earth," or heaven within. They transcend earthly existence and find themselves "seated . . . with [Christ] in the heavenly realms" (Eph. 2:6). This may be understood as the essential meaning of the kingdom of God or of heaven, or "heaven" may replace "kingdom" as the key term for denoting believers' relationship with God. Likewise, this heavenly understanding of the kingdom may be experienced either sacramentally or mystically, or both.

Much rich imagery of heaven has developed primarily (though not exclusively) in the Christian tradition. Such imagery may amplify our understanding of the kingdom of heaven in its more mystical forms. Here the beauties and passions of this life are spiritualized to portray the glory of heaven and of union with God. As noted above, a primary example of this would be Milton's *Paradise Lost.*

Heaven has been variously portrayed down through Christian history—for example, as a paradise garden, a celestial city, or pure light. Some medieval mystics, probably influenced in part by the rising cult of courtly love, pictured heaven in romantic, emotive terms. Colleen McDannell and Bernhard Lang note in *Heaven: A History* that the love mysticism of Bernard of Clairvaux (1090–1153), as seen for example in his depiction of the relationship between the soul and God in *Sermons on the Song of Songs,* "infused medieval Christianity with an emotional dimension and inspired a generation of mystics."[16]

An example of this tradition is the influential medieval German mystic Mechthild of Magdeburg (c. 1207–1282). In one of her visions she sees her soul as a noble lady meeting Christ in heaven. She writes, "The beloved [Mechthild] goes to the most beautiful youth [Christ] and enters the chamber of the invisible deity. There she finds the bed of love" and Christ says to her, "Put away [the garments of] fear and shame and all outward virtue. Keep, in eternity, only those virtues that are inside yourself by nature. They are your noble lust and your ardent desire; to those I will respond eternally in my boundless tenderness." Mechthild responds timidly, "O Lord, now I am a naked soul and you are a God most glorious," and she says, "Our union is eternal life without death." She concludes, "Thus comes to pass what both of them desire: he gives himself to her, and she herself to him."[17] This secret meeting in heaven is a fleeting moment, but it signifies an unending union of hearts.

Here the picture is of God (Christ) as Lover more than as King. But in such mystic visions the Lover is in fact the King. The imagery to some degree reflects the context of the royal court on earth, consistent with the courtly love motif. Thus we really do have here a model of the kingdom, but in a highly mystical, heavenly sense. In this particular example the mystical communion is between the individual soul and God, as in the Interior Kingdom model. Yet, Mechthild, who spoke at times of the "heavenly kingdom," also envisioned heaven in a communal sense.[18]

While the Heavenly Kingdom model is broader than such mystic visions of heaven, this tendency shows how spiritualized the hope of the kingdom may become. Here the pendulum has swung almost totally from the earthly to the heavenly side as physical, sensual delights are transformed into spiritual experience.

ASSESSING THE MODEL

What are the strengths and liabilities of the Heavenly Kingdom model? We may note three points of criticism and three positive values.

One weakness of this model is its narrow biblical basis. It draws on a rather restricted range of scriptural truth compared with some other models, particularly in its more mystical form. On the other hand, much of the New Testament material concerning faith, love, hope, and the fellowship of believers may be interpreted in this highly spiritualized way.

This model is often criticized, second, as an overspiritualization of the reality and the promise of the kingdom. Proponents of this model would contend, of course, that the kingdom is essentially spiritual and eternal and would view any compromise of its radical spirituality as a secularizing trend. But the Bible, particularly in the Old Testament prophetic passages but also in the New Testament, speaks of the material, this-worldly aspects of God's reign as well as its more classically spiritual aspects (as we shall note further when we come to those models that stress the meaning of the kingdom for the present social order). In the polarity between the kingdom as earthly or heavenly, and to some extent in the polarity between the kingdom as future or present, this model loses much of the tension by stressing one side to the loss of the other.

Finally, due to its radical spiritual emphasis this model often shows little concern for, and may see little possibility of, positive social change. This reflects the conviction that the world of time and space, which is passing away, is by nature imperfect and unredeemable. The more highly sacramental forms of this model may actually work against concerns of social reform. In the sacraments, we now participate symbolically but really in the future world, so that is where our attention should be focused. The spiritual, sacramental enjoyment of the reality of God's reign is so important and meaningful that it may largely cancel out any motivation to see the kingdom manifested now in the social order.

This is not to suggest that those who represent this model have no social concern. Often people with a high sense of spiritual reality and communion with God show great compassion for others and seek to meet human need.

They generally do so, however, not to embody the kingdom on earth or to redeem the social order but simply as an expression of Christian love. Also, in some people the Heavenly Kingdom model may be linked with other models that are oriented more toward social transformation.

This model shares with the model of inner spiritual experience a sense of the reality of the unseen world. While it is less individualistic than the Interior Kingdom model, much of the criticism of that model, including its Platonic dualism, may apply as well to this conception of God's reign.

On the other hand, we may say that the weakness of the Heavenly Kingdom model is also its strength. Its profound sense of the reality of spiritual communion is a counterbalance to the materialism that often infects the church. This model knows that the kingdom is fundamentally spiritual, but, unlike the previous model, it knows also that it is profoundly social.

Relatedly, the Heavenly Kingdom model has a strong experiential element. One can actually participate now in the heavenly kingdom, tasting now of "the powers of the coming age" (Heb. 6:5). The kingdom is neither a disembodied ideal nor a merely future hope. It is deep, shared, personal experience through the communion of saints. This has provided profound meaning for millions of Christian believers through the centuries, giving life purpose, direction, and deep inner peace even in very troubled times.

A third and final value of this model is its richly symbolic and esthetic character. It is rich in sacramental sensitivity, which in turn can give it a profound affinity for symbol and thus for various forms of artistic expression. This may be manifested in liturgy, architecture, music, or in other ways.[19]

In sum, the Heavenly Kingdom conception of God's reign is similar to the first model, but is more corporate and communal. It has a profound sense of the inner world, the realm of the spirit. Its sense of sacrament, the mystery of sign and symbol, provides a link with model four, the Ecclesiastical Kingdom.

5 MODEL FOUR: THE KINGDOM AS INSTITUTIONAL CHURCH

I will give you the keys of the kingdom of heaven; whatever you bind on earth will be bound in heaven, and whatever you loose on earth will be loosed in heaven. (Matthew 16:19)

WHAT IS the link between the church and the kingdom? Are they essentially the same or distinct? This is a key question in any attempt to understand the kingdom of God, for its answer largely determines how the kingdom is understood.

The question has been answered in various ways: by sharply distinguishing church and kingdom; by making them identical; by seeing the church as the present form of the kingdom; or, often, by not even raising the question—which usually has the effect of making church and kingdom *de facto* equivalents. The issue is complicated by the question of *which* church one is speaking—"visible" or "invisible"; militant or triumphant; gathered or scattered; the church as institution or as community—and likewise, which form of the kingdom?

An important strand of Christian tradition identifies the kingdom with the church as a visible institution on the earth. Quite simply, the church is the kingdom of God, or at least the present form of the kingdom. This model we will call the kingdom as institutional church, or the Ecclesiastical Kingdom.[1]

The key text for this model is Jesus' words to Peter in Matthew 16:18-19: "You are Peter, and on this rock I will build my church, and the gates of Hades will not overcome it. I will give you the keys of the kingdom of heaven; whatever you bind on earth will be bound in heaven, and whatever you loose on earth will be loosed in heaven." This controversial text, however it may be interpreted, clearly links the church and the kingdom, and includes the element of authority ("the keys"). The text has been central in Roman Catholic ecclesiology, of course, because of its emphasis on Peter. Protestants often claim that the "rock" here refers to Peter's confession of Christ, not to Peter personally. But in either case church and kingdom seem tied together here. The apparently close linking of the foundation ("rock") of the church with the authority of the kingdom makes this a key text for the Ecclesiastical Kingdom model.

In this view God reigns now on earth in and through the church, and particularly through its structures of authority. The visible church is sign, symbol, and representative of God's invisible reign over all things. Thus we may identify three key features of this model: (1) kingdom and church are closely linked conceptually and theologically, often with no distinction being made between the two, particularly in popular piety; (2) the church is viewed especially as the present, visible form of the kingdom; and (3) the authority structures and authoritative claims of the church are especially prominent. Much of the language and symbolism of the kingdom is applied to the church, thus strongly affecting the church's self-identity.

Fundamental images or metaphors of the kingdom in this case are the City of God (an image with both Old and New Testament roots) and the royal priesthood (based on I Peter 2:4-9). This model mines biblical themes that speak of God's people as a kingdom, so naturally the Israelite monarchy during its glorious days under David and Solomon becomes paradigmatic. Passages like Psalm 29:10-11 provide important background:

> The LORD sits enthroned over the flood;
> the LORD is enthroned as King forever.
> The LORD gives strength to his people;
> the LORD blesses his people with peace.

A number of New Testament passages can be interpreted so as to support this model. For example, Revelation 1:6 and 5:10 speak of God's people as "a kingdom and priests" who will "reign on earth." Similarly, Hebrews 12:22-23 says that God's people "have come to Mount Zion, to the heavenly Jerusalem, the city of the living God . . . to the church of the firstborn, whose names are written in heaven."

In the ecclesiastical model the church is seen as the custodian and embodiment of God's reign. God rules over all the earth, at least in a hidden way, and actually and visibly in the church. The agency of God's reign is the church's established leaders (pope and hierarchy in the Roman Catholic model; bishops or other leaders in Protestant variations) and, at the local level, the clergy. In medieval Christendom, kings and the nobility also ruled, especially in secular affairs, but under the ultimate authority of the church. This mentality may carry over into our modern age in the form of high respect paid to Christians who are in positions of social, political, or economic influence. And clergy may be seen as "the Lord's anointed" to rule the church in Christ's stead. A clear distinction between clergy and "laity" is generally a part of this model, partly because of its accent on authority. The fundamental conception seems to be inherently hierarchical and conservative, since God now rules on earth through visible authorized representatives.

MODEL FOUR: THE KINGDOM AS INSTITUTIONAL CHURCH

Many of the theologians and writers cited in this book affirm some kind of essential link between the church and the kingdom, whatever their primary model of the kingdom may be. In other kingdom models, however, it is almost always the "true" church, the "invisible" church, or the church as it gathers in worship that is in view. Only this model goes so far as to identify the church in its institutional or established form as the present kingdom of God on earth.

This model's tendency to identify the kingdom with church structures is often linked with a strong emphasis on sacred space and on the church building as God's temple. The church building is "God's house," the place where God's reign is especially experienced. This is part of this model's tendency to locate God's presence in the life and experience (especially worship) of the church.

Like others, this model has also become enshrined in the church's hymnody. A primary example is the well-known hymn of Timothy Dwight:

I love thy kingdom, Lord, the house of thine abode,
the church our blest Redeemer saved with his own precious blood.

Beyond my highest joy I prize her heavenly ways,
her sweet communion, solemn vows, her hymns of love and praise.

Sure as thy truth shall last, to Zion shall be given
the brightest glories earth can yield, and brighter bliss of heaven.

This hymn shows several of the characteristics of the Ecclesiastical Kingdom model: the identification of the kingdom with the church, the emphasis on worship and sacrament, and the sense that the church is the place or "house" where God dwells. The central focus of God's glory and action is the church.

What are the signs of the kingdom in this model? Obviously the success, growth, and power of the church are viewed as visible evidence of the reality of the kingdom. Thus the prosperity of the church and success in evangelism are often seen as kingdom signs. The signs of God's reign are institutional and sacramental since the church in its life and sacraments signs forth the kingdom. As we noted in the last chapter, a sacramental understanding undergirds both this model and the previous one, providing the link that holds them together in tension.

The opponents of the kingdom in this model are not only Satan and demonic forces but everything that opposes the institutional church as well. Critics of the church in its present form, therefore, are subversive and may easily be seen as heretics. At bottom, heresy is not so much doctrinal error as, above all, refusal to submit to the church's instituted authority. In medieval Catholicism this became defined theologically as the papacy developed in power: To be a member of the true church is to be in union with its earthly head, the pope. Thus failure to submit to the pope is by definition heretical and places one outside the church.

The beneficiaries of the kingdom in this model are all Christian believers—clergy, nobility, and the rest of the "laity"—who share in the blessings of the kingdom now, especially through the sacraments, and will inherit eternal life. The final goal of the kingdom is the evangelization of the world and the extension of the church's authority over all the earth. In more contemporary ecclesiologies that maintain little tension between church and kingdom, the primary kingdom goal is likely to be understood as world evangelism and church growth. The church's mission is to establish bodies of Christian believers among all peoples and gain as many active members as possible.

THE MODEL IN HISTORY

The Ecclesiastical Kingdom model emerges in times when the church is successful or dominant in society. It is not the model of the pilgrim colony traveling toward the heavenly city but of the church more or less at home in its social setting, having developed a certain cultural influence and prestige.

Historically, this model owes much to the influence of Augustine's *City of God*. Augustine (354–430) spoke of the church as God's "present kingdom," and said at one point: "Therefore the Church even now is the Kingdom of Christ, and the Kingdom of heaven. Accordingly, even now His saints reign with Him, though otherwise than they shall reign hereafter."[2] For Augustine the church is much more than its visible institutional expression, and God's kingdom is much more than the church. But his close identification of church and kingdom laid the foundation for a model of the church that makes little or no practical distinction between the two. As the "imperial papacy" developed in the centuries following Augustine, it became quite natural to conclude that the kingdom of God had now come on earth in the form of the church. The logic of this was bolstered as the Roman Empire collapsed and the church became the dominant and shaping force in society.

The view of church and kingdom elaborated in the *City of God* represented a significant shift in Augustine's own thinking. Augustine initially held to a literal millennial reign on earth but abandoned this view about the year 420 as he reflected further on the events of his time. He came to view the "first resurrection" mentioned in Revelation 20 as referring to the Christian's being raised from the death of sin to new life in Christ. The thousand years, then, were to be understood symbolically, not as a millennial reign on earth. Christians now reign with Christ in his kingdom, for they are themselves that kingdom. "Augustine . . . abandoned Millenniarism even in its most refined form, and . . . adopted in its place, on the basis of the biblical distinction between the reign of Christ now and the reign of God hereafter, an identification of the kingdom of Christ with the Church as it now is."[3] As Jaroslav Pelikan notes: "Augustine set the standard for most catholic exegesis in the West when he surrendered the millenarian interpretation of Revelation 20 . . . in favor of the view that the thousand years of that text referred to the history of the church."[4]

Thus in the history of the church after Augustine the kingdom of God came increasingly to be associated with the institutional church. We may think of this model, therefore, as the dominant view of medieval Christianity in the West from about A.D. 500 until the Reformation and, in the case of Roman Catholicism, until Vatican II. In the Roman Catholic tradition, this understanding of the kingdom was embodied in the decrees of the Council of Trent (1545–1563).

In the traditional Roman version of this model, the role of the pope is central. The pope is literally the "vicar" of Jesus Christ, the one who presently rules on earth in Christ's stead. The church is so closely associated with the kingdom that very little distinction is made between the two. Thus the biblical tension between church and kingdom is largely dissolved.

There are also Protestant versions of this model, as already mentioned. Christians in every tradition tend to move toward this view whenever the distinction between church and kingdom is not clearly maintained. Much of Protestantism, particularly at the popular level, in fact often confuses the church with the kingdom. The result is that church work and kingdom work are seen as being the same thing, and the kingdom is reduced in its present form to the dimensions of the church. The kingdom may be seen as much broader, and even as being political and economic in its final, future manifestation, but the church is seen as the present form of the kingdom.

The Ecclesiastical Kingdom model has played a large role in American Protestantism, often in combination with other models. Christians have never been able to establish a theocracy (model six) in the United States, but as Christianity became increasingly dominant and successful it often blurred the line between church and kingdom. How this happened is clarified by recalling the argument made some years ago by sociologist Peter Berger in his book *The Noise of Solemn Assemblies*. Berger contended that the key role played by organized religion in American cultural life amounted to "a *de facto* political establishment of religion." True, "the American state is, indeed, separated from any one religious body, but . . . it is emphatically *not* separated from religion in general."[5] What we have is cultural Christianity:

American society possesses a cultural religion that is vaguely derived from the Judaeo-Christian tradition and that contains the values generally held by most Americans. The cultural religion gives solemn ratification to these values. The cultural religion is politically established on all levels of government, receiving from the state both moral and economic support. The religious denominations, whatever else they may believe or practice, are carriers of this cultural religion. Affiliation with a religious denomination thus becomes *ipso facto* an act of allegiance to the common political creed. Disaffiliation, in turn, renders an individual not only religiously but also politically suspect.[6]

Berger was describing the situation in mid-twentieth-century America. The degree to which his last statements about denominational affiliation no longer hold is a measure of religious and cultural change in the United States over the past thirty years since the book was published. Yet, much of his description remains true.[7]

In such a situation of cultural acceptance of Christianity the distinction between church and kingdom becomes fuzzy. With time even sectarian groups, lacking real persecution, have difficulty placing all the blessings of the kingdom either in the future or in heaven (whether above us or within us). On the other hand, the diversity of groups keeps any one denomination from controlling society, so the theocratic model is not a credible temptation. The Ecclesiastical Kingdom model thus becomes the default option. It may be a largely unconscious option; Christians may not intentionally identify the church with the kingdom, but they easily lose any sense of tension or difference between the two.

In this sense, the model of the kingdom as institutional church has been prominent in much of American Protestantism throughout the last two centuries. The picture is now changing, however, as noted by Stanley Hauerwas and William Willimon in *Resident Aliens: Life in the Christian Colony*.[8] Because of the pluralism and tolerance of American society, the Ecclesiastical Kingdom model has infected not only "mainline" denominations but also more distinctly Evangelical and Pentecostal groups as they have grown and gained cultural respectability (for example, the Church of the Nazarene, the Church of God [Anderson, Indiana], the Assemblies of God, the Free Methodist Church). Often in the move from "sect" to "church" a denomination continues to adhere formally to an earlier futurist, heavenly, or interior model of the kingdom but moves *de facto* and unreflectively to the Ecclesiastical Kingdom model. Ironically, the Roman Catholic Church in North America, finding itself only one "denomination" among many, has progressively moved away from this model toward more countercultural or transformative ones.

The question may be raised at this point as to whether the modern church-growth school, particularly in its more popular forms, holds this view.

C. Peter Wagner, a primary exponent of church-growth thinking in North America, discusses this question in *Church Growth and the Whole Gospel.* He points out the danger of identifying the church with the kingdom but sees "a partial identification" between the two.[9] The church, though imperfect, is the principal agency in the world for proclaiming and interpreting the kingdom. Defining the signs of the kingdom primarily in terms of Luke 4:18-19, Wagner sees both miraculous "signs and wonders" and preaching the gospel to the poor as evidence of the kingdom. While not all church growth is kingdom growth, says Wagner, "The major burden of the Church Growth Movement has been to assist new conversion growth, the kind of church growth that most nearly parallels true kingdom growth."[10] He adds,

> If true kingdom preaching, by the power of the Holy Spirit, makes disciples who become responsible church members, then the growth of the church is very intimately connected with the growth of the kingdom of God. This view avoids, I hope, the danger that J. G. Davies warns against when he says that "to define the goal of mission as church growth is to indulge in an ecclesiastical narrowing of the concept of the kingdom of God." Certainly no church growth advocate that I know would want to be guilty of narrowing either the concept of the kingdom of God or the command for its extension.
>
> As the kingdom of God is preached and more and more people submit themselves to the reign of the king, the wider blessings of the kingdom of God will be more evident.[11]

Though Wagner speaks of a variety of signs of the kingdom, it is clear that he and other church-growth advocates in fact see the numerical growth of the church as the front line of kingdom advance and, therefore, a key sign of the kingdom.

The thesis that the numerical growth of the church is the primary cutting edge of the kingdom of God needs critical examination. Church growth and kingdom growth need to be distinguished in a way that affirms both but does not confuse the two. As Mortimer Arias has written, "Church growth per se cannot be taken as the whole of Christian mission or the overpowering motivation for evangelization. We are not sent to preach the church but to announce the Kingdom."[12] Similarly the late Orlando Costas wrote, "Church growth *is* a sign, a provisional and penultimate goal of the mission of God. In other words, the category of growth is basic to a correct interpretation of the Christian mission in general and the church's evangelizing ministry in particular. The problem, however, is what kind of growth may be associated with the mission of God and what kind of growth may be expected as an authentic result of the church's evangelistic endeavor. While church growth can and must be considered as a sign and provisional goal of the mission of God and a proper fruit of evangelism, not every kind of growth is related to this mission and to evangelism."[13] Implied here is the fact that churches may be faithful or unfaithful to the kingdom, and the growth of an unfaithful church is not particularly good news.

ASSESSING THE MODEL

Like all models, this one has its strengths and its limitations. We may note first three inherent liabilities.

An obvious problem with this model is that it fails to adequately maintain the biblical tension between the church and the kingdom. This failure leads to other problems, as we shall see. Granted, most forms of this model do make *some* distinction between church and kingdom, perhaps seeing the church as embodying the kingdom primarily sacramentally or as the present imperfect form of the future kingdom, or seeing it as the kingdom of Christ, which will finally issue in the kingdom of God. But if the church is identified as the kingdom even in some sort of sacramental or incomplete sense, the tendency is to compromise the prophetic edge of the church.

The second criticism follows from the first. Linking the church so closely with God's reign tends to induce triumphalism and a lack of self-criticism. The church becomes blind to its own faults and intolerant of its critics. The tendency is made worse by the stress on ecclesiastical authority in this model, which can (and often has) led to abuses of power and persecution of opponents. Not only the church but also its structures become sacralized so that proposals for fundamental renewal may be seen as rebellion against God's reign.

A final point of criticism is that the Ecclesiastical Kingdom model tends toward an institutional-hierarchical rather than an organic-charismatic view of the church. As noted earlier, this model seems to be inherently hierarchical and conservative. It easily leads to the abuses for which the monarchical model is often criticized. Thus it can be oppressive rather than liberating; static rather than transforming; stifling rather than enabling. Many Liberationist critiques of the church are often directed toward the problems engendered by views of the church that fail to maintain the church-kingdom tension. Jesus said in Luke 12:32 that his disciples were being *given* a kingdom, not that they were to *be* one. Only in eschatological pictures of the church, such as in the book of Revelation, do we read of the church being made a "kingdom of priests."

Hierarchical and authoritarian understandings of church and kingdom have come under heavy fire from feminist and other Liberationist theologians in recent years. It may be that their critique really concerns fundamentally *this particular model* of God's reign, however, not necessarily all models. Almost by definition, this model tends to lose any prophetic cutting edge as it tilts toward more priestly and/or royal aspects of the gospel. The Ecclesiastical Kingdom model makes an easy target for prophets and radicals.

On the other hand, we may note some values of this model. The sacramental link between the church and the kingdom can be a fruitful one, as the Vatican II document *Lumen Gentium* shows and as Dulles and others have argued—provided the prophetic, eschatological note is kept prominent.[14] The sense of sacramental mystery is central both to the church's life of worship and service and to the presence of God's kingdom in the world.

To guard against triumphalist tendencies, biblical images like suffering servant, flock, community of disciples, and pilgrim people must also be accented. At the center of the throne is the Lamb, "looking as if it had been slain," who does not yet appear as the terrifying Lion (Rev. 5:6). It is precisely in its suffering, brokenness, and refusal to lord it over others that the church most authentically signs forth the mystery of the kingdom. This suggests an even more profound sense of sacrament than triumphalist views of the church often exhibit.

Another value of this model is the impulse it may provide toward world evangelism. Linking the church with the kingdom puts the church's mission in global perspective and urges the church to fulfill its worldwide mission. This impulse itself is valid and biblical, for Jesus directed his followers to "go and make disciples of all nations" (Matt. 28:19) and said, "This gospel of the kingdom will be preached in the whole world as a testimony to all nations, and then the end will come" (Matt. 24:14). The problem is not the church's world vision, which itself is biblical and inherent in the church's identity. The world vision may become arrogant or oppressive, however, depending on the models of church and kingdom by which it is understood. At this point the positive contributions of the Ecclesiastical Kingdom model must be balanced by those of other models.

The church has often been a stabilizing force in society. This model, more than most of the others, seems to be on the side of security and stability. Although this tendency can be negative—depending on the nature of the social order at any particular time—yet we should remember that change for its own sake is not necessarily a positive value. There is something to be said for the church's conservative, stabilizing role in society as long as the church is not party to oppression or injustice. This perspective also suggests perhaps a certain sociological realism about the church that is part of this model of the kingdom.

In sum, the Ecclesiastical Kingdom model is marked by a close identification of church and kingdom, yielding a conception of God's reign that tends to be sacramental, conservative, hierarchical, and often authoritarian. The church easily drifts into this model through the gradual force of traditionalism and institutionalism and through its own success within a given cultural context. The church can guard against the negative aspects of this model by making it secondary to models that are more dynamic and prophetic, grounded in and nourished by the sense of ever-newness that is part of the biblical gospel.

Down through history the liabilities associated with this model have repeatedly provoked reactions in the direction of radical reform in the church and a clear distinction between church and kingdom. This leads us to the fifth model, to be discussed next.

6 MODEL FIVE: THE KINGDOM AS COUNTERSYSTEM

Blessed are you who are poor, for yours is the kingdom of God.
(Luke 6:20)

SOME PEOPLE see the kingdom of God as a "countersystem"—a way of conceiving and organizing society that is counter to its dominant form at present. Usually this view is a protest against the previous model, which tends to associate the kingdom too closely with the church. In the countersystem model, not only is the kingdom distinct from the church, but it is a wholly different way of living and organizing society as well. Here the church is often criticized as being unfaithful, as having compromised its true identity by accommodating to the spirit of the age. We may call this model the Subversive Kingdom, for it consciously seeks to replace society's dominant values and structures with those of God's reign.

This model holds that the kingdom of God is a reality and set of values to be lived out now, in the present order, in radical obedience to the gospel and in opposition to the powers of the present age. Primary images here are the victory of the Lamb and the imitation of Christ understood in a this-worldly, ethical sense.

Four features especially mark the countersystem model. First is its prophetic character. It sees the biblical injunction to seek first God's kingdom and righteousness as a call to justice in society according to the values of the kingdom. Relatedly, this model shows particular concern for the poor and oppressed, the victims in society. It reminds the church of God's special care for the widow, the orphan, and the alien.

Second, this model is strongly Christocentric, especially in its ethics. Most models of the kingdom in some way focus on Jesus Christ, of course, but various models may have quite different understandings of Jesus. This model focuses on the character of Jesus' life and his call to discipleship. It is perhaps the most Christocentric model in this sense, though as we shall see, model seven, the Kingdom as Christianized Culture, also lifts up Jesus as an example. The principal difference is that this conception focuses on Jesus as the center, model, and foundation of the Christian community as a missionary minority in society, whereas model seven hopes to see the values and teachings of Christ thoroughly permeate all of society.

This suggests the third feature of this model: its call to the church to be a counterculture in faithfulness to Jesus Christ. Thus the ecclesiological parallel to the countersystem model is the church as counterculture.

Finally, the countersystem model is the model of the "peaceable kingdom." Christians are to trust God for victory, not to take the sword into their own hands. They renounce violence and retaliation because Jesus did and because of the way God conquered through Jesus Christ. In God's own time and way God will judge the wicked and right all injustice. Historically, advocates of the countersystem model have generally been pacifist as a matter of principle.

The Subversive Kingdom model focuses on Scriptures that speak of God's reign as a new order of peace and justice that is now breaking into the present age. The Sermon on the Mount or Jesus' Jubilee proclamation at the Nazareth synagogue (Luke 4:18-21) may be seen as the charter of the New Community of the kingdom. Jesus instructs his disciples to pray, "Your kingdom come, your will be done on earth as it is in heaven" (Matt. 6:10). He says his followers should seek God's kingdom, knowing that God will supply all their needs, adding, "Do not be afraid, little flock, for your Father [delights] to give you the kingdom" (Luke 12:32).[1] The vision of the triumph of the Lamb in Revelation is a supreme picture of the culmination of the kingdom and provides hope and direction for faithful living now.

Jesus Christ himself—his character, his servanthood, and thus what he reveals about the nature of God who rules over all—is seen as the most profound and convincing basis for the countersystem model. This is the Jesus who says, "The Son of Man did not come to be served, but to serve, and to give his life as a ransom for many" (Matt. 20:28). It is primarily in this sense that one can say that Jesus' kingdom is not of this world (John 18:36). Thus the question of the kingdom focuses on the person of Jesus and on living out Jesus' call to discipleship such as found, for example, in Mark 8:35-38 and 10:29-31.

The countersystem model also draws heavily on the Old Testament. It lifts up those passages that promise *shalom* and call for justice for the poor as the proper response for those who acknowledge God's sovereignty. For

> the LORD reigns forever;
>> he has established his throne for judgment.
> He will judge the world in righteousness;
>> he will govern the peoples with justice.
> The LORD is a refuge for the oppressed,
>> a stronghold in times of trouble. (Ps. 9:7-9)

As Israel's prophets called God's people to repent and live in faithfulness to the covenant, so today the kingdom calls us to the life of servanthood and justice we see in Jesus, consciously rejecting the corrupt or idolatrous values and structures of the present age. Old Testament themes of peace (*shalom*), land, justice for the poor, and the Jubilee, understood as having a present and not just a future relevance, can be enlisted in support of this model of God's reign.[2]

In the countersystem model God rules over all but is opposed by the principalities and powers, visible and invisible, that are in rebellion against God. The church as a missionary minority is seed and sign of the kingdom precisely in the church's weakness and suffering. In its dominant and institutional form, however, the church is in a fallen state and is in fact an obstacle to the manifestation of God's reign. Thus this model and its ecclesiological parallel of the church as counterculture generally posit some view of the fall of the church (usually associated historically with the Emperor Constantine and governmental recognition of the church) and of the need for the church's restitution and restoration.[3]

This understanding of the role of the church in relation to the kingdom is expressed clearly by John Howard Yoder, one of the most articulate advocates of this perspective: "The alternative community discharges a modeling mission. The church is called to be now what the world is called to be ultimately. . . . The church is thus not chaplain or priest for the powers running the world: she is called to be a microcosm of the wider society, not only as an idea, but also in her function."[4]

The Triune God is the agent of the kingdom, not earthly rulers, whether secular or ecclesiastical. Christians in the present do not yet reign with Christ except perhaps in a spiritual sense. Their calling is not to rule but to serve in fidelity to Christ; to be faithful "martyrs" in the original sense of witness, willing to suffer. Ultimately all peoples and all the earth will share in the blessings of the kingdom, but in the present the primary participants are the followers of Jesus Christ, those who make up the faithful community.

The most important sign of the kingdom according to the countersystem model is demonstrated fidelity to Jesus Christ. To the degree that peace, justice, and reconciliation are realized on earth, these also may be viewed as kingdom signs. The final goal of the kingdom is peace and justice on earth and in all creation as God's rule is fully manifested.

THE MODEL IN HISTORY

The church of the first two centuries in its actual life seems to have embodied this model to a considerable degree, though of course with a strong sense of future hope as well. In fact, this is a basic model of the kingdom when Christians find themselves a persecuted or despised minority in society. The model tends to recede as the church becomes prosperous and powerful, but it reemerges in renewal groups that call the church back to its original character. Certainly the Christians in the first century were viewed by many as subversive: "These men who have caused trouble all over the world have now come here" (Acts 17:6).

To a large extent, Augustine understood the kingdom as countersystem in picturing the Heavenly City struggling against the Earthly City. This was still the time of the relative weakness of the church. It was only later, when the church emerged as the dominant force in society, that his thinking became the support for the model of the kingdom as institutional church. Augustine himself was a countersystem thinker. But soon the countersystem became the system.

Perhaps the clearest example of this view is Francis of Assisi (1182–1226) and the early Franciscans. In a radical and simple gospel reaction to the church of his day, Francis set out to embody a new model of the church and of the kingdom. He sought to model the church in gospel simplicity, living out the radical character of the kingdom of God now, in this present age. He thus stressed the present relevance of the kingdom. This is typical of the countersystem model. God's reign is something to be experienced and embodied now in Christian community, in faithfulness to the example and command of Christ and in faith that God himself will eventually bring the kingdom in its fullness.

For Francis, G. K. Chesterton wrote, "Religion was not a thing like a theory but a thing like a love-affair."[5] Francis delighted that God was King over all of life and all creatures. He loved the Lord's Prayer, and prayed:

> Your Kingdom Come:
> So that You may rule in us through Your grace
> and enable us to come to Your kingdom
> where there is an unclouded vision of You
> a perfect love of You
> a blessed companionship with You
> an eternal enjoyment of You.[6]

The kingdom is future and eternal, but also graciously present in the life of the community. So Francis says, "All the brothers should wear poor clothes, and they can patch them with sackcloth and other pieces with the blessing of God; for the Lord says in the Gospel: 'Those who wear costly clothes and live in luxury' (Lk. 7:25) and 'who dress in soft garments are in the houses of kings' (Mt. 11:8). And although they may be called hypocrites, nonetheless they should not cease doing good nor should they seek costly clothing in this world, so that they may have a garment in the kingdom of heaven."[7] Francis was drawn to the Sermon on the Mount, and a key text seems to have been Matthew 5:10: "Blessed are those who suffer persecution for the sake of justice, for the kingdom of heaven is theirs."[8]

Francis said the brothers should acquire no property, money, or goods but rather "as pilgrims and strangers" in the world "serve the Lord in poverty and humility . . . begging for alms with full trust." They should not "feel ashamed since the Lord made Himself poor for us in this world. This is that summit of highest poverty which has established you . . . as heirs and kings of the kingdom of heaven; it has made you poor in the things [of this world] but exalted you in virtue."[9]

It would be misleading to imply that the kingdom was a central theme for Francis; rather the point is that out of his devotion to Christ, Francis and the early Franciscans found a perspective for life in the world that gave the kingdom a present and transformatory relevance. As Regis Armstrong and Ignatius Brady write in their introduction to *Francis and Clare,* "The life of Saint Francis as seen through his writings is one of maintaining a relationship with his Father, of seeking always to do His will, and of making his way to Him after the model of His son." Francis and Clare "responded to the promptings of the Holy Spirit by embracing lives of ever-deepening poverty and humility. And, as a result, they became effective instruments of the Holy Spirit in promoting the kingdom of peace that Christ had come to establish."[10] "In his deep love for the Church," they add, "Francis became a reformer in the fullest sense of the word. He embraced the foundations of the ecclesial tradition and built his own life firmly on them."[11] He became a radical reformer by modeling what the kingdom of God can mean in everyday life and in the present order. His very method of reform was one with his understanding of the nature of the kingdom.

Parallels have often been drawn between the early Franciscans and the Anabaptists, the Radical Reformers of the sixteenth century.[12] The Anabaptists do in fact provide another historical example of this model of the kingdom. Much of the original writing from the Radical Reformation as well as modern reexaminations and affirmations of this tradition breathe the spirit of the Subversive Kingdom model.[13]

In recent decades a considerable literature has appeared affirming and exploring the Subversive Kingdom model. These include Ronald Sider's influential *Rich Christians in an Age of Hunger*; Donald B. Kraybill, *The Upside-Down Kingdom*; André Trocmé, *Jesus and the Nonviolent Revolution*; Mortimer Arias, *Announcing the Reign of God: Evangelization and the Subversive Memory of Jesus*; and Andrew Kirk, *The Good News of the Kingdom Coming.*[14] Several of these books explore the Jubilee theme as a key to understanding the present relevance of the kingdom. These books are typical of the views of many "radical Christians" today who see the kingdom of God as clashing with the values and the view of society that are dominant in the world and often in the church. *Sojourners* magazine fairly consistently articulates this model of the kingdom. It is no accident that *Sojourners* and others with similar views have been drawn to the earlier examples of the Franciscans and the Anabaptists as models, for the logic of church and kingdom is quite similar in all three cases. Some versions of Latin American liberation theology also view the kingdom in this way, though in its more politically activist versions it often represents models we have yet to discuss.

Stanley Hauerwas and William Willimon's 1989 book *Resident Aliens: Life in the Christian Colony* affirms a countersystem model of the kingdom and is significant because it signals a potential shift in models within "mainline" Protestantism. As I suggested in the previous chapter, church bodies that are well rooted within a society, as the historic Protestant denominations are in the United States, with time tend toward culture-affirming views of the kingdom. Hauerwas and Willimon argue that it is time for a new model, as their title suggests.

Jesus' Sermon on the Mount, say these authors, is "the inauguration manifesto of how the world looks now that God in Christ has taken matters in hand. And essential to [this] is an invitation to all people to become citizens of a new Kingdom, a messianic community where the world God is creating takes visible, practical form." This is an eschatological proclamation because it points to God's ultimate purposes. "So discipleship, seen through this eschatology, becomes extended training in letting go of the ways we try to preserve and give significance to the world, ways brought to an end in Jesus, and in relying on God's definition of the direction and meaning of the world—that is, the kingdom of God." The key question, therefore, is: "What sort of community would be required to support" the kind of life "sketched by Jesus in the Sermon on the Mount?"[15] These authors call not for withdrawal from the world but for a level of integrity of Christian community that will by its very nature be distinct from a power-mad, self-centered society. The vision of the kingdom here seems to be that of countersystem.

ASSESSING THE MODEL

In assessing this model we may note some of the points at which it has been criticized. It is sometimes censured for having a negative or pessimistic view toward human culture or for passivity regarding the political process. The contrarian character of this model can result in Christians not taking sufficient advantage of opportunities to influence the political process or to shape culture in constructive ways. The countersystem model is in tension with models six and seven precisely at this point.

The Subversive Kingdom model has also been criticized for failing to appreciate the institutional church. It often has a strong anti-institutional bias that (in some forms of the model) can be sociologically naive about the need for and inevitability of social structures. Sometimes those who criticize bureaucracy and institutionalism forget that every human group necessarily creates structures and that all structures, even new ones, tend with time to become self-serving or stifling. Also, God historically seems to have been able to work in spite of "dead" church structures. Renewal movements often spring up precisely from within the cracks of creaking ecclesiastical institutions.[16]

The countersystem model has several attractive features. We may note four.

In the first place, the countersystem model has prophetic power. It envisions the kingdom as both idealistic and realistic, both as an inspiring vision of the future and as a life that can and must be lived now. This vision serves as a potent spring for active, costly discipleship in the world rather than either hopeless passivity or casual self-satisfaction. The gospel is possible in all its power, and that is a dynamic hope. Historically this vision has been a powerful source of prophetic inspiration in society and has appealed especially to young people.

Second, the countersystem model also can claim considerable biblical support. As we have noted, it appeals not so much to obviously prophetic or apocalyptic passages as to the Jesus Christ of the Gospels. Jesus' life and his call to discipleship are the basis for this model. This view stresses that Jesus preached openly and often about the kingdom. This was his theme; yet, the key to the kingdom is not so much Jesus' teachings as Jesus himself. Jesus is the key to the kingdom. In finding and faithfully following him the church fulfills its true vocation. All other biblical teachings on the kingdom, then, are to be interpreted in the light of Jesus as witnessed to in the Gospels. The book of Revelation is to be seen in this light, and in this light is, above all, a revelation *of* Jesus Christ (see Rev. 1:1).[17]

A third asset of the countersystem model is its strong sense of the church as an actual social community, a "new social reality," a people who in fact share "life together" day by day. The church's communion is not merely spiritual or eschatological. It is a shared life in space and time; a way of living out the gospel together in the midst of present society and history. The church is the messianic community that embodies now, visibly, the prophetic reality of the kingdom. As we have seen, the countersystem conception of the kingdom understands the church as a counterculture or countersociety. Theologically, this sociological necessity of being a distinct community is seen positively, not negatively. The church is *called* to be such a community, and it is precisely in *being* such that Jesus' disciples discover the true nature of the gospel, for where two or three gather in his name, there Jesus is among them (Matt. 18:20).

Finally, the countersystem model provides the basis and impulse for faithful witness. Witness is servanthood, since it is following the example of Jesus Christ. From the perspective of this model, Christians are called not to bring in the kingdom but to serve the King in humble, uncompromising faithfulness and in full assurance that God will bring the kingdom to fruition in his time and in his way. Christians' most effective kingdom witness is Christlike servanthood. This means resisting the temptation to force the kingdom or its values on society, for that would betray its very character as, seen in Jesus. "The weapons we fight with are not the weapons of the world" (II Cor. 10:4). Rather, we are to follow the example of Jesus Christ, for "when they hurled their insults at him, he did not retaliate; when he suffered, he made no threats. Instead, he entrusted himself to him who judges justly" (I Pet.. 2:23).

All the models of the kingdom examined in this book have some conception of witness. The countersystem model, however, puts particular stress on witness as faithful servanthood in the spirit of Jesus, regardless of results or consequences.

The genius of the countersystem model is its affirmation of God's reign as both present and future and as both individual and social without compromising either the power or the gentleness of the kingdom. It is very much the model of Jesus Christ as both the Lion and the Lamb (Rev. 5:5-6). God will conquer and the kingdom will come in fullness, but the mystery of the kingdom is that it comes now through weakness and faithfulness. The countersystem model affirms this paradox. In fact, the paradox provides much of the power of the model. In suffering and weakness, Christ's disciples bear the cross as Jesus did because they know that the kingdom, and they with it, will finally triumph. The cross means weakness and death, but also resurrection and power.

From at least one perspective, this model fits midway between models four and six. While it is a protest against the institutional church model, it shares with that model a concern for the life and form of the Christian community in the present world. It exists in sect/church tension with the ecclesiastical kingdom model, for Christians in the countersystem model clearly are "sects" rather than "churches" in the Troeltschian sense. On the other hand, there are significant similarities between Protestant "sects" and

Roman Catholic orders, as several observers have noted.[18] This is not exclusively a Protestant or an early-church model.

With model six, the Theocratic Kingdom (to be discussed next), the countersystem model shares a concern for Christian witness in society. Many of the issues are the same. But, as we shall see, the two models propose starkly different answers.

7 MODEL SIX: THE KINGDOM AS POLITICAL STATE

*Jesus Christ . . . the firstborn from the dead, and the ruler
of the kings of the earth. (Revelation 1:5)*

IS THE KINGDOM of God a theocracy? In a broad sense it is, for *theocracy* is by definition the rule of God. Generally theocracy connotes the present rule of God in and through the structures of human government, however. In this more restrictive sense, theocracy is a model distinct from other conceptions of the kingdom.

In the theocratic view, God's kingdom provides the values and possibly even the methodology for the social, political, and economic organization of society. Our King is God, not an elected official. The kingdom of God is not to be organized democratically but theocratically. The righteous ones rule in the name of God and unrighteousness is not tolerated. The kingdom is not simply a future reality; it is present now, even if not totally visible and manifest. It is growing and will flower in God's actual reign or dominion over all things within history, before the Second Coming of Jesus Christ. Since God's rule includes the social, political, and economic domains, theocracy itself provides the primary metaphor for this model. This is the Theocratic Kingdom.

We may note three key characteristics of this understanding of God's reign. First is its emphasis on law and its insistence that biblical morality ought to be the foundation for all civil law. Precisely how this is so, or to be worked out, varies considerably in the different versions of the model. This stress on law leads almost inevitably to a focus on God's law in the Old Testament, where all of society was organized according to the Mosaic legal code.

A second characteristic of this model is its stress on the sovereign authority of God as Judge and Ruler. This understanding of the kingdom takes the phrase "kingdom of God" much more literally than do any of the other models we are considering. Sovereign authority is usually the primary category by which God is understood, with other divine attributes being interpreted in the light of God's kingship.

A third key mark of this model is a certain optimism about the church, the coming of the kingdom, and the influence of the church in the world. This optimism can go in a number of directions. It may include the view that eventually all of humankind will be converted, or perhaps that the church will remain a minority but that as God's regents will rule politically as the kingdom of God is established on earth. (This model is thus fundamentally postmillennial, though many postmillennialists would reject it in favor of one of the other models that also affirm the present relevance and transforming influence of the kingdom of God in the present order.)

The theocratic model can take a variety of forms. It can be seen as the rule of the church in society or as God's rule through Christian emperors or other political leaders or structures. God's reign encompasses the entire cosmos, but becomes visible particularly in the political-social order. Generally the church is viewed as in some sense the custodian of society, the representative of God's rule on earth. Thus God reigns through "the righteous." This is the "rule of the saints." Secondarily, God rules through the political structures that he has divinely ordained.

Signs of the kingdom in this model are righteousness in society and God's blessings, including prosperity, on his people. The enemies of the kingdom are Satanic forces as well as political, social, or economic powers opposing God's law. The participants in the kingdom are first of all the church, but all who acknowledge God and his law are also beneficiaries of the kingdom. The final goal is the submission of all things to the sovereignty of God and the formation of a perfected, righteous society encompassing heaven and earth.

For obvious reasons, this model tends to work from Old Testament examples. The kingdom of Israel under David and Solomon is often the paradigm. Israel's godly kings had strong personal faith in God (at least at times) and were chosen instruments for leading God's people and enforcing his law politically as well as spiritually.

Advocates of theocracy have found it possible to enlist some of the Old Testament prophetic passages about God's kingdom to support this view. Passages in Isaiah, for instance, that speak of justice and peace coming on earth can be viewed as finding their literal fulfillment in the gradual transformation of society through the influence of the gospel. Isaiah 9:7 says that the "prince of peace" will

> reign on David's throne
> and over his kingdom,
> establishing and upholding it
> with justice and righteousness
> from that time on and forever.

According to the theocratic model, that reign began with Jesus Christ and is everlasting and is coming to increasing fulfillment visibly in history.

Even the seventh chapter of Daniel, much loved by premillennialists, can be interpreted theocratically. Daniel 7:27 says that after the destruction of the fourth great kingdom (usually identified as the Roman Empire), then "the sovereignty, power and greatness of the kingdoms under the whole heaven will be handed over to the saints, the people of the Most High. His kingdom will be an everlasting kingdom, and all rulers will worship and obey him." Advocates of theocracy understand this prophecy as being fulfilled now through Christ and the church, leading eventually to its culmination with the return of Jesus Christ.

New Testament passages can be interpreted similarly. Texts that speak of the kingdom as being present, and especially Jesus' parables depicting the kingdom as a mustard seed or as leaven (Matt. 13:31-34), may be so viewed. In contrast, premillennial views of the kingdom, consistent with their social pessimism, understand leaven in a negative rather than a positive sense.

Romans 13 may also be seen as providing biblical support for a theocratic understanding of the kingdom, since it says: "Governing authorities . . . have been established by God" (Rom. 13:1). Christians are to pray for rulers, try to influence them, and where possible see that people in government are themselves Christians.

THE MODEL IN HISTORY

The theocratic model of the kingdom gained ascendancy, understandably, following the conversion of the Emperor Constantine in A.D. 322 when the Christian church became allied with the political power structure. It flowered in Byzantine Christianity, especially under the Emperor Justinian (483–565). It appeared that the kingdom of God had literally come on earth. The Old Testament, more than the New, became the primary source for understanding the church and for embodying the kingdom.

In the founding of Constantinople, "the New Rome," in A.D. 330 and the fall of Rome eighty years later many Christians saw the triumph not only of the church but of God's kingdom as well. The Christian historian Sozomen identified the Emperor Theodosius (emperor 379–395) as a new Solomon; the Church of the Holy Wisdom (Hagia Sophia), built in its original form by Constantine, became "under his successor Justinian the Christian answer to the temple of Solomon."[1] Jaroslav Pelikan comments:

> What fell to Alaric's marauding Goths in 410 . . . was "Old Rome," not "New Rome," and certainly not the Roman Empire, which had been assured of its continuity through divine providence by the transfer of its capital from Italy to the Bosporous. . . . "New Rome" . . . had taken over Old Rome's place of honor in the empire and . . . eventually claimed on those grounds to have

acquired also a commensurate standing in the church. The privileged status of New Rome as the city of God's own choosing became a persistent theme of Byzantine polemics against the Latins for a thousand years. The great trauma for the East, therefore, was not the decline and fall of Old Rome . . . but the fall of New Rome a whole millennium later, in 1453. . . . The city of Constantinople . . . had stood, even for the Latin West, as the embodiment of the ideal of the Christian empire and of the continuity of Rome.[2]

THEOCRACY AND THE REFORMATION

The theocratic model was perhaps most fully embodied in Byzantine Christianity—largely because this was politically possible. But we may cite other examples. Geneva under Calvin's dominance has often been described as a theocracy, and "in Calvin's Geneva and Reformed churches everywhere theocratic ideas were prominent."[3] According to Roland Bainton, Calvin felt Christians should

> establish a theocracy in the sense of a Holy Commonwealth, a community in which every member should make the glory of God his sole concern. It was not a community ruled by the Church nor by the clergy nor even in accord with the Bible in any literalist sense, because God is greater than a book even though it contains His Word. The holy community should exhibit that parallelism of church and state which had been the ideal of the Middle Ages and of Luther, but had never been realized and never can be save in a highly select community. . . . Calvin came nearer to realizing it than anyone else in the sixteenth century.[4]

To call Geneva a theocracy during Calvin's presence there from 1541 until his death in 1564 is, however, somewhat problematic. No doubt the church (principally in the person of Calvin) increasingly came to dominate every aspect of society. Yet, Calvin himself did not see this as a theocracy. Formally the city was governed by an elected city council, which was viewed as the legitimate, God-ordained political authority but not as the rule of God or the establishment of God's kingdom. To call Geneva a theocracy is, it seems to me, to misunderstand Calvin. If he himself did not intend a theocracy, clearly he was assuming a different model of the kingdom.

Geneva under Calvin has variously been termed a "theocracy," a "clerocracy," a "bibliocracy," and a "christocracy."[5] Georgia Harkness speaks of "the Genevan theocracy"; yet, she says "bibliocracy" would be more accurate "for it was upon the Scriptures (and by implication upon Calvin's interpretation of the Scriptures) that the whole structure rested."[6] In fact, Calvin taught the structural separation of church and state. He wrote: "The gospel is not to change the administration of the world, and to make laws which pertain to the temporal state. It is very true that Kings, Princes, and Magistrates ought always to consult the mouth of God and to conform themselves to His Word; but our Lord has given them liberty to make the laws which they know to be proper and useful by the rule which is committed to them."[7]

Clearly Calvin did not envisage political leaders making laws *contrary* to Christian truth, for an actual separation between society and the church was as foreign to him as it was to all the magisterial reformers. As W. Fred Graham notes, for Calvin separation of church and state "existed . . . more in theory than in practice. By his words Calvin expressed an ideal of separation; by his practice it is quite clear that separation for Calvin did not mean what it does for most Americans today."[8] Graham summarizes Calvin's view:

> Calvin had a high regard for the honor of the state and its rightful leaders, and . . . his regard for the secular was so great that he did not propose to place the church over it. Yet he saw the church as independent in its sphere, in no way subservient to the realm, the great fault he thought he detected in Germany and England, as well as in the Catholic countries. The two were to exist side by side, serving and ruling the same people with mutual respect and aid. The church did not attempt to prescribe civil laws, nor the state to usurp spiritual discipline. But the church preserved its right to speak *as a church* to the state, not just through the influence it exerted on individual Christians who might be magistrates. It is this last insistence that has called forth the term "theocratic."[9]

Thus Calvin had a generally more positive view of the function of government and of Christians' role within it than did Luther. Government exists not only to restrain evil but also to promote morality and the public welfare. This includes particular care for the poor. "A just and well-regulated government will be distinguished for maintaining the rights of the poor and afflicted," Calvin wrote.[10] All Christians, whether magistrates, church leaders, or common citizens, are to work for the common good.

Thus Calvin's Geneva was not technically or in theory a theocracy—though practically, due largely to the force of Calvin's character within a fairly limited geographical context, it functioned much like one. The intent was simply to have a well-regulated, godly society, not literally to establish God's kingdom on earth. Niebuhr was right to cite Calvin as an example of the "Christ transforming culture" viewpoint.[11] This was Calvin's view of the relation of the Christian faith to society—not so much theocracy as transformation. Yet, for Calvin this was only one—and not the primary—aspect of the meaning of God's sovereign reign. His own theology of the kingdom cannot, therefore, properly be called theocratic. His primary model, as argued in chapter 3, was that of the Interior Kingdom, but with the Future Kingdom and the Transforming Kingdom (to be discussed in the next chapter) as important secondary or corollary models.

The influential Strasbourg reformer Martin Bucer (1491–1551), in some ways a bridge figure between Luther and Calvin, makes an interesting study at this point. His treatise *On the Kingdom of Christ* (*De Regno Christi*), written in 1550 for King Edward VI of England, is one of the few Reformation documents to deal at length with God's kingdom or to propose its actual establishment or "restoration" on earth. Formerly a Dominican monk and an early follower of Luther, Bucer was a tireless worker for unity among the Reformers and reconciliation with Roman Catholicism. The young Calvin spent three years with Bucer in Strasbourg during the time Bucer was leading the Reformation there. According to Wilhelm Pauck, "Calvin's mind was profoundly shaped by what he learned and took over from Bucer."[12]

When Bucer was exiled from Germany toward the end of his life, Archbishop Thomas Cranmer invited him to England to assist with the Reformation there. He was appointed professor at the University of Cambridge but died within two years' time. During these months he was a key adviser to Cranmer and his associates and wrote *On the Kingdom of Christ* as a proposal for a thoroughgoing reform of church and society in England. We will never know what effect his proposals might have had, since Edward VI died in 1553 and was succeeded by his sister Queen Mary I, who restored Roman Catholicism and tried to stamp out the Reformation. There is some evidence that Edward's attempts at reform in education and other areas were influenced by Bucer.[13]

Bucer viewed the kingdom of God as, literally, a Christocracy—the reign of Christ not only spiritually but in every area, including economics and commerce; not only in the future but in the present as well. He was conservative in that he accepted the existing political system but radical in his proposals for instituting a top-to-bottom reformation through the ruling authorities in church and state. He was optimistic that such a reform really could be effected on earth through adherence to the written Word of God and by the power of the Holy Spirit. Bucer put more stress on the work of the Spirit than did other Reformers; there is a noticeable "optimism of grace" in Bucer in contrast to Luther and Calvin.

Bucer's concern was "the fuller acceptance and reestablishment of the Kingdom of Christ" in England. He urged King Edward "thoughtfully, consistently, carefully, and tenaciously to work toward this goal, that Christ's Kingdom may as fully as possible be accepted and hold sway over us."[14] Bucer made no fundamental distinction between the kingdom of Christ and the kingdom of God or of heaven; these terms simply accent different facets of the one rule of God through Christ. Fundamentally it is "the Kingdom of our Lord Jesus Christ, the Kingdom of the Crucified One."[15]

Bucer argued that "it is proper to the kingdoms of the world to use even carnal weapons against evil men. But the Kingdom of Christ fights only with spiritual weapons against its enemies, carnal as well as spiritual."[16] Yet, even within the kingdom of Christ political authorities (though not the church) may legitimately use force to restrain vice and promote the common welfare.[17]

Bucer defines the kingdom as follows:

> The Kingdom of our Savior Jesus Christ is that administration and care of the eternal life of God's elect, by which this very Lord and King of Heaven by his doctrine and discipline, administered by suitable ministers chosen for this very purpose, gathers to himself his elect, those dispersed throughout the world who are his but whom he nonetheless wills to be subject to the powers of the world. He incorporates them into himself and his Church and so governs them in it that purged more fully day by day from sins, they live well and happily both here and in the time to come.[18]

Bucer believed that the fortunes of the kingdom varied throughout history and that "the present time of the Kingdom of Christ is as yet fluctuating and uncertain."[19] Rarely has the church or kingdom enjoyed the prosperity prophesied in Scripture; even in the best of times the "real people of Christ" have never been "so numerous as to cease to be a little flock in comparison with the rest of mankind."[20] The fullest embodiment of Christ's kingdom in history was in the time of the emperors Constantine and Theodosius.[21]

Bucer denied that his proposals constituted an unworkable ideal or "some so-called Platonic republic." Rather, they were the logical outworking of biblical truth that authorities in church and state were bound to promote. Bucer writes in conclusion:

> With the Son of God thus reigning among people of this kind, how could true sanctity and dutiful charity not prevail? They would impel a person always to learn and do some good work so that everyone would contribute his share for the use of the churches; thus the Church would so thrive in each and every member of Christ that no one would be in want, not only of necessary food, shelter, and clothing, but also of any other means of commodity for living well and happily in the Lord, our King Jesus Christ, and in his universal Church.
>
> If, therefore, the one dispenser of kingdoms and powers and the preserver of all, Christ the King, gives to this his people also external sovereignty and a free administration of the commonwealth, because they love and worship this their King "with their whole heart, and soul, and strength" (Luke 16:27), he will give them also all political power and all external strength, so that his Kingdom and his pure and genuine religion may grow and flourish among them and prevail everywhere as fully as possible.[22]

Although one notes affinities between this view of the kingdom and later Puritan views, Bucer's treatise does not seem to have exercised any strong direct influence on later Puritan theocratic visions.[23] Clearly Bucer was advocating a form of theocracy. However, his emphasis on grace, the Holy Spirit, and the need for careful pastoral work softened somewhat the legalism or juridicism that is often a part of this model.

Theocratic ideas of the kingdom were common in sixteenth- and seventeenth-century England as well as in Colonial America. In England the Commonwealth under Oliver Cromwell (1599–1658) was intended to be a literal theocracy. Even more thoroughly theocratic were the Fifth Monarchy Men of Cromwell's day, radical millenarians who interpreted Daniel 7 to mean that God was about to set up a fifth empire (following the Babylonian, Persian, Grecian, and Roman), centered in England, which would rule the earth through his saints.[24]

Regarding the North American scene, H. Richard Niebuhr notes that "taken literally, the establishment of theocracy was not the hope of the Puritans only. It was no less the desire of Pilgrims of Plymouth, of Roger Williams and his assorted followers in Rhode Island, of the Quakers in the middle colonies, of German sectarians in Pennsylvania, of the Dutch Reformed in New York, the Scotch-Irish Presbyterians of a later immigration and of many a native movement."[25]

This raises the question of theocratic ideas in the formation of the United States. Was the new North American republic seen as an attempt to embody the kingdom of God? It seems clear, as Sherwood Eddy wrote in *The Kingdom of God and the American Dream,* "that many of the founders and builders of the new world, though they had not yet formulated the American Dream in the colonial wilderness, were motivated by deep religious convictions and that their aim was often expressed in terms of the Kingdom of God as their ideal."[26] Such an ideal might or might not take the form of theocracy, of course, but the ideal of the Theocratic Kingdom was certainly a key ingredient in the mix that produced the United States.

Historian Arthur Schlesinger, Jr., argues that United States history should be understood as an ongoing "warfare between realism and messianism, between experiment and destiny," and that these elements provide the key to understanding the repeated "cycles of American history."[27] The messianic strain tended to attach itself to the hope of the kingdom of God. "Independence gave new status to the theory of America as an 'elect nation' (Bercovitch) or a 'redeemer nation' (E. L. Tuveson), entrusted by the Almighty with the charge of carrying its light to the unregenerate world," writes Schlesinger. "The Kingdom of God was deemed both imminent in time and immanent in America. It was a short step from salvation at home to the salvation of the world."[28] He notes that Harriet Beecher Stowe could speak of "the glorious future of the United States . . . commissioned to bear the light of liberty and religion through all the earth and to bring in the great millennial day, when wars should cease and the whole world, released from the thralldom of evil, should rejoice in the light of the Lord."²⁹

In spite of such visions, theocracy did not prevail in the United States, largely because of the religious and philosophical pluralism that had already developed by the time of the American Revolution. No one group had the clout to enforce theocracy, and many leaders rejected any theory of government that could too easily become repressive or autocratic. It appears that the chief legacy of the theocratic model was to reinforce the idea that Americans were in some sense a chosen people. That vision became secularized and yet continues in the popular view that the United States is destined in some sense or other (ideologically, culturally, or economically) to rule the earth.³⁰ Yet, with this vision there has always been also in American history the more modest and pessimistic (or realistic) countercurrent that sees the republic as a precarious experiment.

CHRISTIAN THEOCRACY IN CHINA

That the theocratic vision is no respecter of persons or cultures is seen in the remarkable story of the Taiping Revolution in China in the 1850s. A poor young Chinese scholar by the name of Hong Xiuquan (1814–1864) learned of the Christian faith through a series of tracts published by a Chinese evangelist associated with the pioneer Protestant missionary Robert Morrison. Hong converted to Christianity and later saw himself as God's special emissary, a sort of second Christ, sent by God to establish *Taiping Tienkuo,* the "Heavenly Kingdom of Eternal Peace and Prosperity." Hong made many converts, formed the Society of God-Worshippers, raised a large popular army, and within a few years gained control of nearly half of China in his attempt to drive the Manchus from power. He established his capital at the important city of Nanjing.³¹

Hong Xiuquan appears to have been a remarkable charismatic leader. He proved to be a more effective visionary and insurgent than administrator or political leader, however. His movement lost momentum shortly after its administrative capital was established. Strategic military errors on the Taiping side and the eventual involvement of Western powers in support of the Manchu government in Beijing brought defeat by the mid-1860s. Hong himself died of illness and malnutrition in Nanjing in 1864, his capital besieged and his kingdom disintegrating. Yet, for a decade he ruled over much of China in a movement that has come to be seen as "the first chapter of China's century of revolutionary struggle."³²

Though Hong Xiuquan had only a very rudimentary understanding of Christianity, clearly the primary inspiration for his movement came from his vision of God as heavenly King and Father and of Jesus Christ as the

Son who died to redeem the world from sin. The peculiar amalgam of his views traces in part to a series of visions he had before reading the Christian tracts. In his visions he saw a venerable old man and his middle-aged son and received a commission to rid the world of demon worship. When Hong later read the Christian tracts, he was amazed to find his visions confirmed. He identified the old man of his visions with God the Father and the son as Jesus Christ. Hong thereafter saw himself as the Younger Brother of Jesus, sent to earth to establish God's kingdom.

Hong had a few weeks' contact with Southern Baptist missionary Issacher J. Roberts, from whom he learned something of the Scriptures and of Christian worship and organization. But he soon departed to fulfill his divine commission. Jen Yu-wen notes: "It was only after his complete conversion to the Christian faith...that his consciousness of kingship by appointment from God and his assignment to the sacred task of overthrowing the imps, i.e. idols and Manchus, became an idée fixe."[33] Yu-wen adds: "Taiping Christianity was in reality a new sect manifesting orthodox and heterodox elements as well as indigenous influences. In common with Christians everywhere, the Taipings worshiped God, acclaimed Christ the Savior, read the Bible, followed the Ten Commandments, performed baptism, and believed in heaven and hell."[34]

Hong apparently understood God more as law-giver than as gracious Savior. He seems to have taken the Fatherhood of God in a literal rather than symbolic sense and to have rejected the doctrine of the Holy Spirit. Jesus Christ is God's Son, but not himself God. Fundamentally Hong's conception of Christianity seems to have drawn more on the Old Testament than the New, with an ethic that was more moralistic and legalistic than love-centered. He stressed that Jesus' coming did not abolish the law.

Hong Xiuquan understood God's kingdom as a literal earthly theocracy, as his annotations on Scripture make clear. Commenting on Matthew 5:13-48, from the Sermon on the Mount, Hong says:

> To speak of one great kingdom is to include both heaven above and earth below. In heaven above there is the Heavenly Kingdom [*Tienkuo*]. On earth below there is the Heavenly Kingdom. Heaven and earth both are the Spiritual Father's Heavenly Kingdom. Do not make the mistake of believing that this indicates only the Heavenly Kingdom in heaven. Therefore the Elder Brother's prophecy says: "The Kingdom of Heaven approaches." For this Kingdom of Heaven will come on earth. It is the Kingdom of Heaven which the Heavenly Father and Heavenly Elder Brother [Jesus Christ] now have descended to earth to establish.[35]

On the prophecy of Jesus' return in Acts 1:10-11, Hong comments, "Now Christ has come down into the world. It is fulfilled." In interpreting Revelation, Hong left no doubt as to the identity of the New Jerusalem: "The new Jerusalem sent down from heaven by God the Heavenly Father is our present Heavenly Capital. It is fulfilled" (on Rev. 3:12).[36]

Hong Xiuquan and his movement have received varying assessments. Jen Yu-wen believed that had the revolution and its projected social reforms succeeded, "Christianity translated from revolutionary creed to state religion would have initiated a new spiritual life among the people at large and brought abrogation of noxious social customs and all superstitious practices" and transformed China into a modern industrial state. As it turned out, he noted, "the Taiping uprising touched off fifteen tragic years of bloody conflict that was unprecedented for sheer destructiveness and cost many millions of lives in nineteen provinces." Historically it served as "forerunner of the National Revolution of 1911."[37] In an 1853 essay titled "Revolution in China and in Europe" Karl Marx spoke of the "chronic rebellions subsisting in China for about ten years past, and now gathered together in one formidable revolution" in the Taiping movement.[38] Because of his revolutionary and egalitarian ideology, Hong Xiuquan is considered a national hero by Chinese Communists. The noted China scholar John King Fairbank wrote: "Taiping Christianity was a unique East-West amalgam of ideas and practices geared to militant action, the like of which was not to be seen again until China borrowed and Sinified Marxism-Leninism a century later."[39]

Christian interpreters have tended to see the Taiping Movement as a tragically missed opportunity. W. A. P. Martin wrote in 1897 that "an opportunity was lost such as does not occur twice in a thousand years."[40] Kenneth Scott Latourette felt that the Taiping Movement gave Christianity a bad name to some extent; yet, its socially destabilizing effect in areas where it was strongest may have "weakened the resistance to Christianity and so partly prepared the way for the foreign faith."[41]

Even though quite syncretistic, Taiping Christianity provides a good example of the theocratic model. It was a thoroughgoing attempt to set up God's kingdom on earth. It exhibited that combination of sense of divine commission and willingness to use force which often makes this conception of God's reign politically unsettling.

THEOCRACY TODAY?

The theocratic model has resurfaced in recent years in some influential ways. The view of the kingdom implied in the agenda of the Moral Majority a decade ago and expounded in Pat Robertson's 1982 bestseller *The Secret Kingdom* is in some respects a theocratic vision. Robertson says he and many others "are now discovering this central purpose of our Lord . . . the kingdom of God." Christians "should reach from the visible into the invisible and bring that secret kingdom into the visible through its principles—principles that can be adopted at this moment" and which have clear socio-political implications.[42] This view tends to see the United States as a nation uniquely blessed by God and charged with a mission to promote and safeguard God's kingdom and free-enterprise capitalism throughout the earth. These are not conflicting goals, for in this view capitalism is the economic system most compatible with, and uniquely blessed by, the values of the kingdom.[43]

The model of the kingdom as political state is most radically articulated today by so-called Reconstructionist or Dominion Theology advocated by R. J. Rushdoony, David Chilton, Gary North, and others. Reconstructionists call for reorganizing society on the basis of Old Testament civil law. Crime and immorality would not be tolerated; God's rule would be enforced. Dominion Theology has been set forth in a spate of books over the past twenty-five years, and more recently has been picked up by a number of independent Charismatic leaders, especially in the South and West of the United States. It is sometimes called "theonomy" because of its stress on the "law of God." William Barker and Robert Godfrey note that in recent years "this school of thought has produced a vast amount of literature, influenced the Christian-school movement, affected many churches, and stimulated some previously quietistic evangelicals to political activity."[44]

The philosophical basis for Reconstructionism was set out by Rushdoony in several books, particularly his *Institutes of Biblical Law,* first published in 1973. David Chilton, perhaps the most popular Reconstructionist author, has written: "The Bible gives us an eschatology of dominion, an eschatology of victory. This is not some blind, 'everything-will-work-out-somehow' kind of optimism. It is a solid, confident, Bible-based assurance that, before the Second Coming of Christ, the gospel will be victorious throughout the entire world."[45] As an eschatology of dominion it is also an eschatology of law. Another Reconstructionist author, Greg Bahnsen, argues that "every jot and tittle of the Law of Moses, with the exception of the ceremonial code, is binding upon mankind today."[46] Clearly the theocracy envisioned in Reconstructionism is more a kingdom of law than of grace.

In their critique of Reconstructionism, Barker and Godfrey point to the theocratic issue. The key hermeneutical question, they suggest, is how "the Israelite theocracy under the Mosaic law [is] to be understood and its typological significance related to the proper role of the church and of the state today."[47] They summarize the chief characteristics of Dominion Theology as:

> an emphasis on the Old Testament law; stress on the continued normativity not only of the moral law but also of the judicial law of Old Testament Israel, including its penal sanctions; and belief that the Old Testament judicial law

applies not only to Israel, but also to Gentile nations, including modern America, so that it is the duty of the civil government to enforce that law and execute its penalties. Christian reconstruction hence has the appeal of claiming to apply biblical principles to contemporary society in a way that will express the dominion of Christ. Usually, Christian reconstruction is characterized by a postmillennial eschatology.[48]

Dominion Theology reportedly had some influence politically in the Reagan White House. The views of North and Rushdoony were circulated among some of Ronald Reagan's key advisors, and a few of Reagan's conservative Christian economists were reading reconstructionist economic theology as they sought to enact the legislation of the "Reagan Revolution."

It is easy to see how this kingdom vision has had appeal to a certain element of the Charismatic Movement, even though the foundational Reconstructionist thinkers are not Charismatics. Charismatic leaders who have been attracted to this viewpoint represent that element of the movement that is politically conservative, that emphasizes taking authority or dominion over the powers of Satan, and that believes that it is God's will for his people to prosper. There is, of course, some irony in Charismatics, with their stress on grace (*charis*) and spiritual gifts (*charismata*), being so attracted to a theology of law.

Among the Charismatic Reconstruction thinkers identified by Hal Lindsey is Joseph Kickasola, professor of international affairs at Pat Robertson's Regency University. The affinity between the Reconstructionist vision of the kingdom and the views set out by Robertson in his book *The Secret Kingdom* is clear from the discussion of Robertson's views above.[49]

At one level, Reconstructionism may be understood as a radical postmillennialism. It is roundly criticized from this perspective by best-selling premillennialist author Hal Lindsey in his book *The Road to Holocaust*. Lindsey charges also that Reconstructionists are implicitly anti-Semitic because they believe God's covenant with the Jews has been canceled and totally transferred to the church, the New Israel.

ASSESSING THE MODEL

The popular attractiveness of the theocratic model is its stress on the immediate relevance of the kingdom and its critique of those who see God's kingdom as being totally future. It is completely understandable that theocracy should present itself as a plausible answer to people of faith who are sincerely concerned with this-worldly dimensions of the kingdom. Since God is sovereign over all and desires his will to be done on earth, theocracy may seem to be the logical answer. However, we may note several points of criticism.

First, this model has meager New Testament support. There is little or no evidence in the New Testament that Jesus intended to set up a "rule of the saints" in society. In fact, Jesus sharply disappointed many of his followers precisely at this point. To support this model biblically one has to rely heavily on the Old Testament, which in turn raises the question of in what senses the Old Covenant is fulfilled in the New. The tendency is to make the Old rather than the New Covenant normative in society.

Theocracy thus yields a kingdom more of law than of grace, as we have seen. This is in part the fruit of interpreting the New Testament in terms of the Old rather than the other way around. Given this hermeneutical twist, proponents of this view often are able to argue for the setting up of the kingdom by force rather than by grace and moral persuasion.

Third, this model may be criticized for overemphasizing God's sovereign rule and playing down other aspects of the character of God. The model generally places little emphasis on the Holy Spirit and the role of the Spirit in society and in the church. When Charismatic Dominion thinkers and preachers emphasize the Holy Spirit, they do so almost exclusively in terms of individual Christian experience. This model also has little room for the suffering Christ. The focus is on the triumph of Christ and, by extension, a triumphant church.

Fourth, the question may be raised as to whether this model exhibits a certain naivete regarding structural evil in society. It assumes that evil and injustice would be done away with if God's order as given to us in Scripture were implemented politically.

An inherent problem with theocratic visions is that God must have some human agency through which to rule. Unless this is the whole community, as in some of the many utopian experiments down through history, these regents are fallible individuals with their own blind spots, vested interests, and philosophical presuppositions. This tends to skew the way God's rule is in fact applied, generally leading to injustices. Yet, attempts to have the whole community rule often collapse for lack of clearly defined authority.

A final criticism is that the theocratic model generally manifests a certain insensitivity toward the poor. In their stress on law and structure, advocates of this model assume that poverty would be eliminated through the institution of theocracy. The model often argues that poor people are poor primarily because of their own indolence.

On the other hand, some positive features of the theocratic model may be noted. First is its concern with the sociopolitical order. Unlike more otherworldly views, this model believes the kingdom has present-day relevance and ought to be visibly manifested in society.

A second value of the theocratic model is its insistence on the importance of moral values. We live in a moral universe; God has revealed in Scripture

God's own character, which provides a permanent moral basis for society. This element can serve as a healthy antidote to more pluralistic or relativistic views that see morality as being, at root, merely psychological or sociological.

Finally, this model has a certain popular appeal because of its confidence that the gospel can be applied in the present social order, as already noted. The model's optimism and assurance about building a just society seem to provide concrete answers to the difficult question of how kingdom values can be incarnated in culture.

The theocratic understanding of the kingdom is similar to models four and five, the Ecclesiastical Kingdom and the Subversive Kingdom, in that it sees God's rule as having present relevance in society. Yet, it differs radically from these models in its understanding of the fundamental character of the kingdom and how it is to be manifested. On the other hand, the theocratic model is like the next model we are to consider, the kingdom as Christianized culture, in arguing that God's reign is a socially transforming reality and that the kingdom comes gradually now, not in some future cataclysm. But as we shall see, the model of the kingdom as Christianized Culture sharply differs from the theocratic model at other points.

8 MODEL SEVEN: THE KINGDOM AS CHRISTIANIZED CULTURE

My servant . . . will not falter or be discouraged till he establishes justice on earth. (Isaiah 42:1, 4)

THROUGHOUT HISTORY many Christians have taken the kingdom of God as a theme, stimulus, or program for the transformation of society. In contrast to otherworldly views of the kingdom, these advocates of social transformation see the kingdom as already present, at least embryonically, and as giving us both inspiration and direction for Christianizing the social order. Several of the models discussed here share this stress on the present reality of the kingdom.

Especially is this true of the model we turn to now: the Kingdom as Christianized Culture. This is preeminently the model of the Transforming Kingdom. Here the kingdom is seen not merely as present, or as the inward experience of believers, but as an active, dynamic principle of social reconstruction empowered by God's Spirit. In this model the kingdom is present, not just future; social, not just individual; and material, not just spiritual.

This model may be seen as similar to the previous one but with a broader range of political and economic options. Rather than a theocracy, the kingdom is a set of values and principles to be lived and applied now in society. Christians are to be transformers, not a countercultural enclave. In this view, the kingdom in its fullness would mean a culture fully leavened by Christian values.

The metaphor of leaven fits both this and the countersystem model, for both see the kingdom as an active transforming agent in society. A better metaphor for the model of the kingdom as Christianized Culture, therefore, might be *enlightenment*. The kingdom progressively illuminates humankind, overcoming fear and ignorance, bringing a better world. It comes gradually, not cataclysmically.

Three key features of this model concern relevance, transformation, and optimism. First, the transformative model stresses the present social relevance of the kingdom, often in conscious contrast to more otherworldly views. The kingdom is a present social reality much broader than the church, for God intends nothing less than the redemption of the entire social order. This model has a strong ethical focus, concerning itself with living out the moral values of the kingdom.

Second, this model accents social, political, and economic realities and processes. It protests conceptions of the gospel that so stress spiritual and religious concerns that they neglect human suffering and oppression. In this view the kingdom of God is a social program, the logical and necessary outworking of the gospel of Jesus Christ in society. The individual and interior dimensions of the kingdom are merely the foundation for complete social transformation. Thus to restrict the gospel to religious experience or to the church is to do violence to the full message of the kingdom.

Third, this model is optimistic about social transformation. The power of the gospel can bring a world of peace, justice, and harmony now, within history. This model tends to be optimistic about the possibilities of just government and equitable social structures and about the church's role in social reform. Whether this optimism is really grounded in the gospel (an "optimism of grace") or is simply borrowed from the particular historical context is an issue meriting further exploration.

The kingdom as Christianized culture is a model of hope, a model that sees the kingdom as God's program for bringing all things on earth into conformity with the divine will. Generally this model sees God's reign as becoming progressively manifest in the present order and as coming by human action cooperating with God's action. This is in contrast to premillennial and other futurist views that tend to see the kingdom as coming primarily or exclusively by God's action and cataclysmically rather than gradually.

The transformative model thus puts particular emphasis on human agency and effort. Responsible human action is seen as playing a key role in bringing the fullness of the kingdom, though God's providence or Spirit is the primary agent. Signs of the kingdom are justice and peace in society and the success of reform efforts. The beneficiaries of the kingdom are to be all humankind and the whole earth. Ignorance, superstition, and oppressive or outdated social structures are viewed as primary obstacles of the kingdom.

Old Testament prophecies of a coming age of peace and harmony (*shalom*) form a key part of the foundation of this model. The vision of peace and cosmic reconciliation so prominent in the prophet Isaiah, and the calls for social justice in the minor prophets, are especially central here. The hope of the kingdom as Christianized Culture is perhaps best captured in such passages as Isaiah 11:1-9, 42:1-7, and 61:1-11.

Few New Testament passages seem to speak of the kingdom as a program of social transformation, though Jesus' parables of the leaven and the mustard seed may be understood as presupposing this model. Often, however, proponents of this model point not so much to Jesus' statements about the kingdom as to the life he lived and the social ethics he taught. Thus the Sermon on the Mount (Matt. 5–7) and even more the somewhat parallel passages in Luke (6:20-26) are important, for they show what it means to live the life of the kingdom. Likewise, the theme of Jubilee and Jesus' apparent allusion to the Jubilee in Luke 4 ("to preach good news to the poor . . . to proclaim the year of the Lord's favor," vv. 18-19) are important for understanding the nature of the kingdom.

THE MODEL IN HISTORY

The kingdom as Christianized Culture has been at least a subtheme in Christian reflection on the meaning of God's reign throughout much of church history. As a distinct model it has come to prominence, however, within the last few centuries. In twentieth-century North America it has been especially influential in "mainline" Protestant seminaries.

Though generally not acknowledged, some of this influence traces back to the German Pietist movement. Johann Albrecht Bengel (1687–1752) and August Hermann Francke (1663–1727), both Pietist scholars, represent the Transforming Kingdom model, though in somewhat different ways. Francke became a major educational reformer as well as philanthropist, missions pioneer, and church reformer. Though Pietism is often criticized for focusing narrowly on inward spiritual experience, Francke and Bengel, especially, worked to transform society after the Pietist model. From his base at the University of Halle, Francke launched a series of educational reforms which clearly had in view the transformation of all of German society, not just the Lutheran Church.

Johann A. Bengel, well-known for his *Gnomon of the New Testament* and other writings, is often viewed as one of the founders of modern biblical textual criticism. He gave considerably more attention to eschatology than did Francke. His writings show that he was postmillennial in viewpoint, expecting the kingdom of God to come in fullness before the Second Coming of Christ. He worked out a detailed "apocalyptic chronology" that culminated in the year 1836.[1]

Bengel's postmillennialism was taken over at least nominally by John Wesley, as Wesley's *Explanatory Notes Upon the New Testament* shows. Although it is clear that Wesley saw the kingdom in its present form primarily as inner spiritual experience, as we have previously noted, he felt strongly that Christians should work to transform society as an expression of impartial love for all people. Wesley himself modeled this, actively supporting a number of reform efforts, including the Society for the Reformation of Manners and the abolition of slavery. He also believed that culture was gradually being transformed through revival and the general spread of the gospel, as several of his sermons indicate. In this sense, Wesley, like Bengel and Francke, represents the Transforming Kingdom model.

To the degree that the transformative model in its various embodiments deals with the question of the millennium, it is generally postmillennial. Because this model sees the blessings of God's reign as promises for the present age, not solely for a time following Jesus' return, it is the model most closely linked with postmillennialism. Postmillennialism may also take theocratic form, however, as we have seen, and advocates of the kingdom as Christianized Culture may as easily hold an amillennial as a postmillennial view.

Postmillennialism generally views the kingdom as a Christianizing reality in society. The grace of God and the power of the kingdom are presently at work, particularly through the church as God's people in the world. Thus society is increasingly being leavened by the gospel, more and more reflecting the kingdom of God. This was a common view among many mid-nineteenth-century Evangelical reformers and revivalists in the United States, including abolitionist evangelists like Charles G. Finney.[2]

Early twentieth-century advocates of the Social Gospel represent a similar view, though in a different way. Nineteenth-century Evangelicals were hopeful about the manifestation of God's kingdom on earth, but never lost sight of its transcendent spiritual, eschatological dimension. In the Social Gospel, the pendulum gradually swung more fully toward a present and earthly conception of the kingdom, losing something of the balance and the biblical tension between present and future.

In the United States, the Social Gospel movement of the early twentieth century constituted perhaps the most fully elaborated example of the Transforming Kingdom model. While the history of this movement traces back to a number of currents (both Evangelical and liberal; both religious and secular) in the previous century, its fullest and most articulate expression is found in the writings of the Baptist theologian Walter Rauschenbusch (1861–1918).

The year 1910 conveniently symbolizes the split between the Social Gospel and Fundamentalism, for in February of that year the first book bearing the title "social gospel" and the first volume of The Fundamentals appeared. Shailer Matthews's little book *The Social Gospel* contended that the gospel was both individual and social in its scope and that Jesus' teachings should be applied in all areas of life. The Fundamentals series contended, on the other hand, in the words of the 1878 Niagara Bible Conference Creed: "We believe that the world will not be converted during the present dispensation, but is fast ripening for judgment, while there will be a fearful apostasy in the professing Christian body, and hence that the Lord Jesus will come in person to introduce the millennial age."[3]

It was in this milieu that Walter Rauschenbusch developed his own understanding of the gospel of the kingdom. Donald Gorrell writes:

> Advocates of social Christianity generally were involved in the emerging struggle between the two contending viewpoints of evangelical Protestantism that were beginning to become quite distinct. Beneath the teachings of social-gospel leaders was an understanding of biblical truth that rested heavily on the teachings of the prophets and Jesus and that pointed to the establishment of the kingdom of God on earth. Since this goal seemed to play down the second coming of Christ and the establishment of a millennial kingdom, many conservative evangelicals felt that the social gospel was denying the basic tenets of Christianity. While the differences had begun to become openly apparent by 1910, they had long been latent in American Protestantism. Already in the 1890s Walter Rauschenbusch was distinguishing his social understanding from that of millenarian Baptists, feeling that their views were an unhistorical way to interpret the Bible, were pessimistic and antiworldly, and were so centered on catastrophes that faith and action became disjointed. . . . The Christianization of the social order taught by social-gospel proponents stood in direct conflict with such millennial teachings of the fundamentalists.[4]

Rauschenbusch articulated a kingdom gospel of social transformation in a number of influential books, including *Christianity and the Social Crisis* (1907) and *A Theology for the Social Gospel* (1917). "The Kingdom of God is humanity organized according to the will of God," he wrote.[5] "The Kingdom of God is the true human society; the ethics of Jesus taught the true social conduct which would create the true society."[6] The kingdom is both personal and social, for "the greatest contribution which any man can make to the social movement is the contribution of a regenerated personality."[7]

"The Kingdom ideal contains the revolutionary force of Christianity," Rauschenbusch contended. "When the doctrine of the Kingdom of God is lacking in theology, the salvation of the individual is seen in its relation to the Church and to the future life, but not in its relation to the task of saving the social order." Rauschenbusch distinguished between the church and the kingdom. He critiqued the church's self-preoccupation and institutionalism. When the kingdom focus is lost the church focuses on itself. "The Kingdom of God breeds prophets; the Church breeds priests and theologians."[8]

In a personal testimony given in 1913, Rauschenbusch told of his own conversion in his youth and how later, about the age of twenty-five, "through personal contact with poverty" he began to wrestle with the social implications of the faith. He was particularly troubled by the needless deaths of little children: "Why did the children have to die?" He soon made the discovery that "the idea of the kingdom of God" was "the real solution" for the problem of the gospel's social witness, for the kingdom is an overarching social conception.[9] "One of the most persistent mistakes" of Christians, he wrote, "has been to postpone social regeneration to a future era to be inaugurated by the return of Christ."[10] Rauschenbusch's pilgrimage parallels in interesting ways that of William Booth of the Salvation Army, who about 1888 came to the conclusion that salvation was "for both worlds"— "for time as truly as for eternity."[11]

The Social Gospel as articulated by Rauschenbusch and others had considerable impact both in the churches and in American society. Because of the Fundamentalist-Modernist split, it was largely rejected by many theologically conservative Protestants who by this time had lost touch with the social-reform character of the Evangelicalism of a century earlier.

One prominent Christian, well rooted in conservative Protestantism, who made a personal discovery of the kingdom theme in a way quite parallel to Rauschenbusch's, was the famous Methodist missionary to India, E. Stanley Jones (1884–1973). Jones makes a useful example because of his marked shift to an emphasis on the kingdom of God in the light of the challenge posed by Communism in the 1930s. Like Rauschenbusch, Jones came to see the kingdom as a theological and practical framework for transforming both individuals and society according to God's will.

On a visit to Moscow during his return trip to India in 1934, Jones was challenged by the vigor of people building, as they saw it, a new world through Communism. Did Christianity have such a hope for society? Or was it only future, inward, and individual? Jones wrestled with this for months, gradually concluding that the kingdom was God's plan and program for all of creation; that it was the true realism. He later wrote, "I had to go outside my native land to make a major discovery—the discovery of the Kingdom of God. I found it, of all places, in Russia! . . . I had always known it, but there it became vital and all-compelling."[12]

The result of this rethinking was Jones's book *Christ's Alternative to Communism,* which called for a fresh application of the gospel of the kingdom in society. Taking Jesus' Jubilee proclamation in Luke 4 as his starting point, Jones outlined what he saw as Jesus' program for "the kingdom of God on earth." Jesus' quoting of Isaiah 61 shows the true nature of the kingdom:

1. Good news to the poor—the economically disinherited.
2. Release to the captives—the socially and politically disinherited.
3. The opening of the eyes of the blind—the physically disinherited.
4. The setting at liberty the bruised—the morally and spiritually disinherited.
5. The Lord's Year of Jubilee—a new beginning on a world scale.
6. The Spirit of the Lord upon me—the dynamic behind it all.

I believe that here we have the outline of the program which [Jesus] intended to project into the soul of humanity. Here he put the first content and meaning into the Kingdom of God on earth.[13]

Jones said the kingdom was as revolutionary as Communism, but unlike Communism it worked from within, not without; by moral persuasion, not by force. But the kingdom is also radically different from capitalism, for its principle is cooperation, not competition. The kingdom of God means "radical change," bringing "human equality and the sharing on an equal basis of the rights and privileges of life for all."[14] This is good news for the poor, and not just in a spiritual sense: "When we do not know what else to do with a thing, we spiritualize it."[15] God's kingdom is both material and spiritual; both inward and outward. The task of the church is to get beyond its trifling concerns and faithfully proclaim Jesus and the kingdom. "I am deeply convinced," wrote Jones, "that Christianity has within it the program and the vitality for the remaking of the world, if we would discover it and apply it."[16]
David Bundy notes that in this book, Jones

drew heavily upon Marxist social theory and Jones' experience in India as it endeavored to describe the "Kingdom of God." *Christ's Alternative to Communism* was a radical document calling for the abolition of repressive structures and the reformation of the world social and economic orders. He urged that alternatives to exploitative capitalist competition be found . . . [and] called upon the Church to reform its goals and structures and to make a more prophetic stance over against injustice and its worldly self-interest.[17]

Jones articulated this theme (on the basis of Heb. 12:28 and 13:8) as "the Unshakable Kingdom and Unchanging Person," Jesus Christ, for the true gospel centers in both the Person and the Plan. He wrote, "I came out of Russia with three life convictions indelibly impressed on me . . . namely: the Unshakable Kingdom, the absolute order; and the Unchanging Person, the absolute person; and both of them are realism—the ultimate realism."[18]
Jones wrote in 1936:

What is the Spirit's voice for this troubled and distracted age searching for a way of life and plans for the future? The Kingdom of God on earth! He is unfolding the possibility of a new world on God's plan. This Plan haunts the councils where all plans are being examined. We are not ready to take the Plan yet, for we are not ready for salvation. We will stumble along until one day we shall fall on our knees and take God's Plan and then! A new age, a new world, a new brotherhood, new men![19]

Jones's understanding of the kingdom was much like Wesley's in its stress on inner experience, but it had a stronger accent on the present reality of God's reign as something to be embodied now, subverting and transforming the present order. Wesley spoke of the kingdom of God, as we have noted, but for him it was most fundamentally inward, associated with the experience of Christian perfection. Wesley focused more on Christian experience than on the kingdom and understood the latter in terms of the former. In Jones's case we can discern a sort of paradigm shift from Christian perfection to the kingdom. The kingdom, or rather, as he always insisted, *Jesus Christ* and the kingdom, became his central theme. He shifted from understanding God's reign in terms of personal sanctification to understanding Christian experience in terms of the kingdom. Elements of futurity are found in Jones, but this aspect is less strong than in Wesley and is more related to the present time than to the ultimate future.

Jones's model seems to be fundamentally that of the Transforming Kingdom—though it might also be called the "implicate kingdom," for Jones saw the kingdom as the true realism, the way God has designed things to work. The kingdom is a fact, something built into human nature and the created order. It will be realized in society when humanity stops struggling against it and, through Christ, begins cooperating with it.

There is thus a social radicalism in Jones's kingdom theology, though this became eclipsed through the popularity of his many devotional books and the tendency of North American readers to take Jones's writings as spiritual inspiration rather than social program. David Bundy suggests that given Jones's "radical socio-economic, political and religious agenda," he should properly be recognized "as the proto-liberation theologian" of the Wesleyan Holiness tradition.[20]

The question of the relationship of Christian faith to culture is, of course, the central theme in H. Richard Niebuhr's influential book *Christ and Culture,* first published in 1951. Though Niebuhr sets forth five types (Christ against culture; the Christ of culture; Christ above culture; Christ and culture in paradox; Christ transforming culture), his book has been widely seen as tilting toward the Christ transforming culture model. Thus Niebuhr may himself be seen as representing the model of the kingdom as Christianized culture.

ASSESSING THE MODEL

The Transforming Kingdom model has at least three significant strengths. First is its optimism and motive power for social change. Generally this model is a conscious critique of "otherworldly" viewpoints that see the kingdom as irrelevant in present society or, worse, as encouraging passivity and discouraging Christian action toward the public good. This model, like others that stress the present rather than the future aspect of the kingdom, provides hope and motivation for some significant coming of the kingdom now, in the present social order.

A related strength of the transformative model is that it sees positive value in human culture. In its insistence that the kingdom is present and social, not just inward and individual, this model stresses the good in human nature, in human cultural achievement and often in the physical environment. Rather than merely a "kingdom of darkness" or a negative drag on the higher, nobler realm of nonmaterial spirit, the world in this view is a place of beauty and value within which Christians add their efforts to perfect society and heal its diseases.

Third, this model stresses human action and responsibility. God has made us responsible creatures, capable actors in the world's drama. Not to accept this role is to fail to seek first God's kingdom and its justice. Sin is not just acts of personal immorality; it is failure to accept God-given responsibility for this world. The worst sin is waiting passively for God to act, for God intends to work through us. Denial of our stewardship of the world is, in effect, a denial of God.

On the other hand, this model has some liabilities. It has been criticized for having a relatively weak biblical base, though as we have seen the hermeneutical grounds for this model are broader than a focus simply on those passages that speak explicitly about the coming of the kingdom of God or the end times. A major element of the biblical basis for this model is, in fact, the argument from creation: God created everything good and commissioned humankind to care for it. We should value all that God has made.

We may point to more substantial limitations of this model, however. It may overemphasize human action, creating the impression that the kingdom of God can be achieved by human activity or through the political process. This is a criticism that was often raised of the Social Gospel Movement, though the clearest exponents of the Social Gospel maintained the balance of divine and human action and of individual experience and social transformation. In the polarity between God's action and human action, however, this model always runs the danger of hubris or humanism, a danger that must be accounted for in any careful articulation of the kingdom as Christianized culture.

Second, there is the question of ecclesiology, the nature of the church. The transformative model often has difficulty in showing how the church is to be an agent of the kingdom. It may too easily see a particular political program as the sure highway to the kingdom. How is the kingdom, in this model, the mission of the church? It is easier to show, for instance, how Jesus' words to his disciples translate into the work of evangelism than it is to show how they translate into the work of social transformation. A biblical and theologically strong case can be and at times has been made for the gospel as social or cultural transformation, but the case involves more complex and indirect argumentation than the simple call to evangelism.

In its concern to transform society, then, this model may have a meager ecclesiology. It may see the church as little more than the means (or even an obstacle) to the end of social reconstruction. Partisans of this view are often impatient with the church, with its conservatism and institutionalism, in their zeal to make the gospel relevant to the great issues of society. Here the transformative model clashes sharply with the countersystem model. Both focus on the present meaning of the kingdom, but the one sees the kingdom coming in weakness through the faithful believing community, while the other sees it coming either in spite of the church or through the church's sociopolitical activity. One frequently sees this tension today in the contrast between the social vision of those with Anabaptist roots or sympathies and people in the Reformed tradition. The context from the sixteenth-century Reformation is still with us in this respect.

Because of its concern with society and with the social and ethical values of the kingdom, this model runs the danger of a culturally bound Christianity. The concern with culture easily leads to an affirmation of one's particular culture, especially if that culture is viewed as already being Christian, or Christianized, in some fundamental sense. This has happened especially in North America. It is all too easy to view the United States as a beacon, a "city set on a hill," radiating God's truth and needing only the continuing infusion of God's light to fulfill its divine purpose—not fundamental, radical reordering. Precisely for this reason, perhaps the countersystem and transformative views of the kingdom need each other. Together the two views may help to maintain the polarities between divine and human action, cultural affirmation and cultural criticism, and the church's stance of being in but not of the world.

Finally, the Transforming Kingdom model may have an inadequate view of sin. How deep does the moral problem of society and of individual men and women go? The Bible presents humankind as deeply flawed morally because of sin, even though created in God's image. This moral taint extends to all human action and creativity, and therefore to all human cultural works. Here is the root of the debate as to whether changing society means first changing individuals or the other way around, and of questions of "legislating morality." The more sophisticated advocates of this model, including proponents of the Social Gospel and some liberation theologians, have insisted that sin is both a matter of the heart and a question of social structures. The tendency of this model, however, is to overlook or underestimate the personal, spiritual, and psychological depths of human sin in its focus on social transformation or cultural betterment. This is in obvious pendularity with views that so fixate on human depravity that they ignore structural evil or consider the cultural question irrelevant.

The kingdom as Christianized Culture resembles the previous model, the Theocratic Kingdom, in its concern for society and politics and in viewing the kingdom as coming incrementally rather than cataclysmically. The concern with culture also places this model close to the final one we will consider, the Kingdom as earthly utopia, in spite of some key differences. All three of these models, as well, are optimistic concerning the possibilities of the kingdom in the present order.

The models of the kingdom considered in this book vary between optimism and pessimism, particularly with regard to the social order. Troubled, uncertain times seem to bring forth apocalyptic visions of the kingdom that are pessimistic about the present but ultimately optimistic. Such visions arise especially among people who are suffering or who are the victims of society. In contrast, more optimistic models of the kingdom emerge in contexts where positive change seems possible and ideas of progress are prominent.

Since Scripture contains passages on both sides of this divide, biblical support can be found for both "optimistic" and "pessimistic" views of the kingdom. This may be another basic polarity regarding the kingdom within Scripture itself. One may hypothesize that in interpreting the Scriptures people tend to be drawn primarily either to "optimistic" or "pessimistic" passages, depending on their social context. Here again we face the issue of hermeneutics in developing a biblical theology of the kingdom.

The most radically optimistic kingdom vision is the final one that we will examine: The Kingdom as earthly utopia.

9 MODEL EIGHT: THE KINGDOM AS EARTHLY UTOPIA

> *The wolf will live with the lamb,*
> *the leopard will lie down with the goat,*
> *the calf and the lion and the yearling together;*
> *and a little child will lead them. (Isaiah 11:6)*

A MAP OF the World that does not include Utopia is not worth even glancing at."[1] Coined by Sir Thomas More, the word *utopia* is a pun based on two Greek words; it can mean either "good place" (*eutopia*) or "no place" (*outopia*). As a dream of what the earth can be or a blueprint for the ideal community, utopian visions point the way to the future. In his survey of literary utopias Lewis Mumford notes, "Almost every utopia is an implicit criticism of the civilization that served as its background."[2]

In Western culture, utopian visions and experiments take their rise both from classical Greek visions of a Golden Age and from the biblical hope of the kingdom. They may be either religious or secular, though at the deepest level they are always religious in that they imply a philosophy of life and embody ultimate values. In popular usage *utopia* suggests a vision of the perfect society but one that is fundamentally impossible, an "impracticable scheme of social regeneration."[3]

To utopian visionaries, of course, proposals for social regeneration are not impracticable; they are often considered highly workable and, in some cases, even inevitable. Utopians see themselves in tune with the future. What makes them religiously and culturally significant is the contagious power of their visions and the way attempts to embody them have affected world history. The most notable example next to the Christian hope of God's kingdom is Communism.

The kingdom of God may be understood as an earthly utopia—a perfect society on earth rather than a "heavenly city." As a model, this view may be seen as the Transforming Kingdom model taken to an extreme. It is literally utopian, envisioning society perfected and at peace with nature. This is a "kingdom" in a symbolic, not a literal sense, for the model tends to envision a classless society with no or very limited government. "God reigns" in a largely passive sense, as the hand of Providence or perhaps some evolutionary force. This view tends to see evil as primarily or exclusively environmental, so that changing the social environment in the proper way can bring a perfect world. We may call this model the Utopian Kingdom.

Three marks of this model may be noted. First is its strong visionary character. This is the most idealistic of the eight models in its vision of earthly society and its optimism about what can be accomplished through human effort.

Second, this model often embodies the ideal of a "Golden Age" to be experienced by humanity. This may be influenced by secular or Greek ideas of a Golden Age in the past or be associated with an evolutionary view that society is progressively moving toward perfection.

Third, proponents of this model often attempt to build a utopian community or society as a prototype of the age to come. Much of the utopian literature (secular or Christian) models what such a community should look like. A good contemporary secular example of this is B. F. Skinner's novel, *Walden II*.

Western culture has spawned a wide variety of utopian visions. Many of these are either a blending of Christian and non-Christian motifs or have been developed as critiques of or alternatives to Christian views of the future (as found, for example, in the first three models we examined). Thus the Utopian Kingdom is often a hybrid model, drawing on a variety of sources in addition to Scripture and the Christian tradition. (This, of course, is not totally unique to this model; as we have seen, other models have been influenced by Greek philosophy and ideas as well as other sources.)

Many of the same Old Testament prophecies of an age of peace and harmony that serve as sources for model seven, the Transforming Kingdom, can also be enlisted in support of this model. Prophecies of peace and reconciliation certainly describe a vision of society that is far beyond what is experienced anywhere in the world today.

An image that captures many of the elements of this model is the New Jerusalem. As it appears in Revelation 21 and 22, the New Jerusalem is the eschatological community where suffering and pain are gone and all is peace and harmony. To be of service to the utopian model, however, the vision of New Jerusalem must be used rather loosely or elastically.

The early church in Jerusalem following the Day of Pentecost (Acts 2–5) can also be a source for this model. The New Testament description of the early Christian community is a powerful vision that, when contrasted with the present-day church or society, can release powerful energy for change and renewal.

As a largely secularized version of the kingdom hope, this model focuses on the earth or the human environment as the locus of the kingdom. The church may be viewed either as an ethical society that embodies kingdom values, or perhaps as irrelevant or an obstacle to the kingdom to the extent that it diverts attention from this-worldly to otherworldly concerns. The agency of the kingdom may be seen as the force of history, Providence, or some evolutionary current drawing humanity to the realization of the ultimate vision. Humanly speaking, the agents of the kingdom are those visionaries who show the way to the future and expand our consciousness and our hope for the utopian dream.

Are there any "signs of the kingdom" in this model? Depending on how the model is shaped, evidence of the kingdom's coming may be seen in the spread of love, goodwill, or global consciousness, or perhaps in the success of utopian experiments. The enemies of the kingdom are traditionalism, ignorance, or entrenched powers that work for self-interest. Opponents may be the rich who horde wealth and undercut the kind of egalitarian communalism which this model often envisions, socioeconomic and political structures, or society itself.

In this kingdom vision the final goal is a perfect, harmonious, balanced society on earth in which there is peace and economic justice. Those who now embody this vision are the participants in the kingdom, but potentially all of humanity, and the whole earth, receive the kingdom.

THE MODEL IN HISTORY

The Utopian Kingdom model finds resonances in the many utopian communities, whether Christian, secular. or a blending of the two, that sprang up in the United States and, to a lesser degree, elsewhere during the nineteenth century. These social experiments are in part the fruit of changes brought about by the Industrial Revolution and the utopian literature it spawned. "A whole group of utopias sprang out of the upturned soil of industrialism," notes Mumford.[4]

More than one hundred utopian communities involving more than 100,000 men, women, and children were formed in North America in the 1800s. Mark Holloway writes, "Fleeing from the industrial problems of Europe, utopian socialists tried to solve them by setting up model societies in America. Thus it came about that the nineteenth century in that country was the golden age of community experiments." "Instead of trying to change society from within," he notes, these utopians "tried to set up models of ideal commonwealths, thus providing examples which (in some cases) they hoped the world would follow."[5]

The utopian community as a substitute for or a secularized version of God's kingdom can be illustrated in the community of Skaneateles, founded in 1843 by John A. Collins on a 350 acre farm in western New York State. Collins, an associate of William Lloyd Garrison in the antislavery cause, was one of several abolitionists who sought solutions to society's ills through forming radical communities. In 1840 Collins made a trip to England, where he was appalled by the economic slavery of laborers that he witnessed there. While in England he talked with the reformer and communitarian Robert Owen and studied socialist tracts. He soon concluded that "war, slavery, and intemperance, are but the effects of some cause lying further back"—namely, "individual ownership in the soil and its products . . . which makes man practically an enemy of his species."[6] From that point on private property functioned in Collins's thinking as humanity's original sin.

In a statement of principles issued in the forming of the Skaneateles community Collins expressed the hope that the benefits of his experiment might be "ultimately secured to all the inhabitants of the globe." Religion or belief in special revelation would have no place in the great endeavor "to work out this great problem of human redemption." Collins wrote:

> While we admire the precepts attributed to Jesus of Nazareth, we do not regard them as binding because uttered by Him but because they are true in themselves, and best adapted to promote the happiness of the race; therefore we regard the Sabbath as other days; the organised church as adapted to produce strife and contention rather than love and peace; the clergy as an imposition; the Bible as no authority; miracles as unphilosophical; and salvation from sin, or from punishment in a future world, through a crucified God, as a remnant of heathenism.[7]

Though Collins's community and his paper, *The Communitist,* were shortlived, they illustrate the Utopian Kingdom model.

We find a similar secularizing of the Christian vision in Étienne Cabet and his Icarian communities in the 1840s and 1850s. Mark Holloway writes:

> It is incorrect to call the Icarian community non-religious. Theirs was simply a more radical interpretation of Christ's teaching than had usually been made. Christ was regarded as the First Communist, a mortal being like other men; supernatural phenomena were not admitted; but the conception of the Deity was retained. "We like to think of God as the father of the human race [Cabet wrote], humanity as His family, men as His children and brothers held together by brotherly love"; and although some Icarians regarded themselves as agnostics, their publications proclaimed that they should love God above all—God being taken to represent "*Justice, Bonté, l'Amour, la Vie.*"[8]

Similar visions have recurred frequently in various forms down through church history in "the pursuit of the millennium."[9] In yet a different way, the utopian model was at work in the founding of the United States, in the sense that the founders rejected theocracy or traditional monarchy for what may be seen as a secularized, politically realistic version of the hope of Christ's kingdom. Thomas Jefferson and Benjamin Franklin, for example, were "utopian" not in the classical sense but in the sense that they put their efforts into building the ideal society on earth rather than the church or the kingdom of God.

The primary modern-day version of this vision has been Marxist Communism. Marxism is perhaps best understood as a secularized, materialistic version of the Christian hope of the kingdom. Despite its practical failures, the great appeal of Marxism has been its vision of a harmonious classless society—a vision that in many of its features is clearly biblical, as E. Stanley Jones argued. This has probably been the major reason for the appeal of Marxism. Conversely, Marxism's failure to achieve this vision led first to disillusionment and finally to the disintegration of Communist political power which the world has witnessed in the last decade of the twentieth century.

Most liberation theologies have a conception of the kingdom that reflects this model, the Transforming Kingdom model, or something in between. That is, liberation theology hopes to see society transformed now into (or according to the values of) the kingdom of God. The Christian's calling is to be involved in the liberating process, with high realism about the social, economic, and political dimensions of the present order. Thus the attraction of liberation theology (in some of its forms) to Marxist analysis is quite understandable. Like Marx, liberationists would be disdainful of "utopian socialists" and might consider themselves "scientific socialists"; yet, at base the vision is that of the Utopian Kingdom model.

Liberation theologies seek a new society of justice and equality, though the means to attain this and the degree to which salvation or the kingdom are identified with political liberation varies. Avery Dulles notes: "Liberation theologians say in effect that the word of God is distorted and alienating whenever it is accepted without commitment to the praxis oriented toward the Kingdom of God. But if we are authentically committed to the Kingdom, we shall be involved in the struggle to subvert the existing social order, with its institutionalized injustice, and to establish on earth a just, fraternal society."[10]

The Peruvian Roman Catholic Gustavo Gutiérrez, whose seminal book *A Theology of Liberation* was first published in Spanish in 1971, argued that building the just society is kingdom work, though the kingdom transcends our efforts. He writes:

> Temporal progress—or, to avoid this aseptic term, the liberation of man— and the growth of the Kingdom both are directed toward complete communion of men with God and of men among themselves. They have the same goal, but they do not follow parallel roads, not even convergent ones. The growth of the

Kingdom is a process which occurs historically *in* liberation, insofar as liberation means a greater fulfillment of man. Liberation is a precondition for the new society, but this is not all it is. . . . Without liberating historical events, there would be no growth of the Kingdom. But the process of liberation will not have conquered the very roots of oppression and the exploitation of man by man without the coming of the Kingdom, which is above all a gift. Moreover, we can say that the historical, political liberating event *is* the growth of the Kingdom and *is* a salvific event; but it is not *the* coming of the Kingdom, not *all* of salvation.[11]

Liberation theologies are generally more insistent on the need for the present radical transformation of society, on the centrality of economics and politics, and on the key role of the poor than are previous models that also wish to see society transformed. The more that particular theologies of liberation focus on this-worldly liberation in reaction to or negation of salvation in narrowly spiritual terms, the more fully they fit the utopian model.

In a starkly different way, the utopian model is also the view of the kingdom found in modern premillennialism. The premillennialism of most North American Fundamentalism, for instance, combines this model with the model of the kingdom as inner spiritual experience (model one) or as heaven (model two). The kingdom has no present-day relevance in this, the "church age," but it will in the future following the return of Christ, when the kingdom comes very literally to earth in the millennial reign of Christ. The millennial reign is to be decidedly literal, political, and earthly. This will be followed, after a thousand years, by the saints' eternal enjoyment of heaven.

Viewed from this perspective, Marxism and Fundamentalism have much in common. The vision of the kingdom is quite similar; the main difference concerns how the kingdom comes. In premillennialism it comes almost entirely by God's action, whereas in Marxism it comes almost exclusively through human action, or perhaps through human action cooperating with or reflecting the inexorable forces of history. Both of these views dissolve the tension between divine and human action and so are to that degree inconsistent with a central aspect of biblical narrative.

A curious mutation of the model of the kingdom as earthly utopia appears in the so-called "prosperity gospel" that has grown up in the United States in the last few decades. In this view the kingdom of God is ultimately future, but since we are children of the King we may even now enjoy the blessings of royalty—materially as well as spiritually. A major problem with this view, in addition to its lack of scriptural support, is that it has little or no place for the cross. The argument is that Christ suffered so that we would not have to suffer, rather than the biblical view that Christ not only suffered for us but also left us an example that we might follow in his steps (I Pet. 2:21).

Formally, much feminist theology fits the utopian model, particularly in its emphasis on equality and community and its strong critique of patriarchal and hierarchical power in the church. Its attempt to build small communities of solidarity among women and to network with others of like mind is typical of this model.[12]

Sallie McFague has argued the case for "an earthly theological agenda" in a way that exhibits several of the features of the utopian model. Her attempts to "deconstruct and reconstruct" the church's "traditional patriarchal, hierarchical, militaristic imagery" of God and salvation imply the rejection or at least radical reinterpretation of the very concept of kingdom or monarchy. She critiques "the dualistic, hierarchical mode of Western thought" as being inherently destructive of the natural world and oppressive of the powerless, because in this approach "a superior and an inferior are correlated: male-female, white people-people of color, heterosexual-homosexual, able-bodied, physically challenged, culture-nature, mind-body, human-nonhuman. In whatever ways we might reconstruct the symbols of God, human being and earth," she writes, "this can no longer be done in a dualistic fashion, for the heavens and the earth are *one* phenomenon, albeit an incredibly ancient, rich and varied one." This new agenda will "turn the eyes of theologians away from heaven and toward earth"; or more accurately to the material heavens and earth viewed as one ecosystem.[13]

McFague argues that the key theological issue now is "not only how we can change the world but how we can save it from deterioration and its species from extinction."[14] The human focus here ("we") is consistent with the model. In most kingdom models the question is not how "we" can save the world but how God saves the world or possibly how God saves people out of the world.

The explicit shift in focus here from the heavenly to the earthly, the radical critique of "dualism" with its implicit questioning of divine transcendence, and the accent on collegiality and ecology mark this perspective as utopian in the sense of our model. Other models may see God's kingdom as an ecological reality but not in so exclusively a this-worldly sense, as we shall see in chapter 11.

In this context we may mention the cosmic vision of Pierre Teilhard de Chardin. Teilhard's views to a large degree represent this model, but probably fall more fully within the model of the kingdom as mystical communion, understood in a cosmic sense. He admitted to being utopian, saying: "It is finally the utopians, not the 'realists,' who make scientific sense. They at least, though their flights of fancy may cause us to smile, have a feeling for the true dimensions of the phenomenon of man."[15] Teilhard's thought has some significance when seen in the long development of views of the kingdom over many centuries. A number of aspects of his thinking, includ-

ing its optimism, its evolutionary assumptions, and its scientific and ecological interest, make it attractive to many as we enter an age of highly
increased global consciousness.[16]

ASSESSING THE MODEL

The strength of the utopian model is its visionary power. Precisely
because of its clash with present reality *and* its insistence that the kingdom
is not an otherworldly future hope, this model can appeal powerfully to (at
least) a significant minority in society. This is true as well, of course, of
some of the earlier models we have examined. The model may appeal especially to people who are turned off by institutional Christianity or traditional religious forms, for it seems to be saying something genuinely new
and yet hopeful.

Also, this model accents the powerful prophetic kingdom visions in
Scripture, particularly in the Old Testament prophets. Taking these Scriptures symbolically and heuristically, this model points to a present translation into reality of the poetic prophetic visions of peace. These elements
give this model a popular appeal that can be socially powerful.

We may note, however, several difficulties with the utopian model.
Although it may draw some poetic inspiration from Scripture, as a model it
has in fact rather meager biblical support. Rather than maintaining the tension of the polarities we noted at the beginning, it is almost entirely an
earthly, present model in which the New Age is brought about through
human action. The aspects of divine action and of the spiritual future
dimensions of the kingdom either disappear or are reconstructed in some
sort of evolutionary, ecological, and/or sociopsychological fashion, which
may seem to fit modern sensibilities but are reductionist of the biblical
worldview.

Relatedly, this model often compromises the uniqueness of Jesus Christ
as the central Person in the kingdom and the one through whom people participate in kingdom life. In E. Stanley Jones's terms, it is an attempt to have
the Plan without the Person on whom it depends. Either Jesus Christ is irrelevant in this model, or "Christ" is a sort of cosmic goodwill with no necessary or essential connection to the historical Jesus. Jesus may be seen as a
fine historical example or paradigm of the kind of life that the kingdom
envisions, but little more.

The meagerness of the biblical basis in this model is seen also in a kind of
naivete regarding human nature. The Utopian Kingdom has little place for
sin as a personal moral contamination or bentness. Sin is often seen primarily as a matter of unjust social structures, unhealthy relational patterns, or
cultural traditions. In some forms of this model the reasoning is: People are

good; social structures (or at least the presently dominant ones) are bad. Salvation or the way to the kingdom, therefore, means demolishing or modifying structures so that innate human goodness may flourish. This may be understood in an economic class sense, as in Marxism, or in a more sociopsychological sense, as in some New Age thinking.

Human sinfulness is no respecter of persons. Divide up people as we will— rich and poor; black and white; male and female; "liberal" and "conservative"; "materialist" and "spiritualist"; "New Light" and "Old Light"— the line of personal selfishness, self-seeking, and willingness to inflict or condone the suffering of others cuts across all categories and runs through every human soul or psyche. This model (and perhaps others as well, though the moral equation may be differently defined) generally fails to recognize the internal depth of human self-centeredness and thus tends to be naive about the perfectability of human nature and society apart from the fundamental work of God's grace through Christ within the human spirit.

Finally, we may note two points of comparison between this and other models. The Utopian Kingdom may be seen as model seven, Christianized Society, secularized and taken to a this-worldly extreme. It naturally has some points of similarity with the previous model in its concern for culture. Both models focus on present society: human life on earth now.

The second point of comparison is with model one, the Future Kingdom. As our final model, and as the end of the continuum from future to present and heavenly to earthly, the Utopian Kingdom is at the farthest extreme from the kingdom as future hope. But as we have already noted, the two models envision remarkably similar pictures of what society may or will become. They differ radically as to the means and the aspects of the character of the final goal, but the utopian and futurist visions themselves are quite similar: a human society of peace, harmony, beauty, health, and equality. So in a sense the two ends meet to form a circle. The future will be golden.

10 KINGDOM MODELS AND CHRISTIAN FAITHFULNESS

THE EIGHT MODELS outlined in this book present different options for resolving the six biblical tensions or polarities listed in chapter 1. Though I have not done so in detail, one could systematically critique the strengths and weaknesses of each of the models according to how they handle these points of tension.

If we take Scripture seriously, we must affirm that the kingdom is *both* heavenly and earthly; *both* present and future; *both* individual and social. That is the nature of God's reign because of who God is and because of the nature of the created order. The kingdom comes *both* by divine and human action, yet without compromising God's sovereignty. The kingdom comes gradually, but there are those crisis points, those critical moments of powerful inbreaking or revelation of the kingdom. The Bible consistently presents the day of the final coming of the Son of Man as the crowning cataclysm. Finally (as we have seen), the kingdom is not the church but is closely linked with the church because Jesus Christ, the one under whose sovereignty all creation is being gathered together, is also Head of the church (Eph. 1:9-23). The church, to the degree that it is faithful to Jesus Christ, is the first fruits of the kingdom, of the general reconciliation God is bringing to fullness.

If the eight kingdom models were plotted along a single continuum, "earthly utopia" might be at one extreme and "heavenly city" at the other. The kingdom as institutional church would then fall approximately in the middle, as would the model of the kingdom as countersystem. The kingdom as political state would be closer to the "earthly utopia" side, while the kingdom as mystical communion would be nearer to the "heavenly city" side.

In reality, however, the picture is more multidimensional than such a continuum would suggest.

What do these models mean for us today? The challenge is to be clear about our models and to critique them by Scripture. We can learn also from the experience of history.

No one of these models is fully biblical or fully adequate. But several of them do embody key truths of the kingdom as taught in Scripture that need to be reflected in a usable contemporary biblical theology of the kingdom. As we move increasingly into a one-world society, it is crucial that Christians articulate and embody such a vision of the kingdom, and accordingly an experience of the church that is consistent with this vision.

COMPARING THE MODELS

One could analyze and "rate" the eight kingdom models by systematically comparing them with the six polarities noted in chapter 1. Each model might be assigned a number or range of numbers along the axes of the six polarities, according to where they seem to fit. A continuum for each polarity might be devised as follows:

$$1----2----3----4----5-----4----3----2----1$$

Thus, for example, on the present/future axis a model that is dominantly present or dominantly future would receive a 1 or 2; a model that is at midpoint between the two would receive a 5; while a model that combines the two in tension might receive a 13 (4+5+4) or even a 19 or a 23 (2+3+4+5+4+3+2). If this calculation were carried out along all six axes for all eight models, one would have a numerical rating for each model of, say, from 6 to 138. Obviously this formula is biased toward valuing those models that most inclusively maintain a tension in all six polarities and against those that do not, and especially against those that fall fairly exclusively *either* to the one side or to the other of the polarity. This bias, however, is consistent with the thesis suggested in chapter 1, that the most useful and biblically faithful models are those that best maintain the tensions of the polarities.

The advantage of this formula is that it further clarifies the differences between (and similarities among) the models in terms of the six tension points posited. It allows one to argue for greater overall usefulness of some models compared with others. The obvious problem with the formula is that it gives an impression of quantifiable objectivity that may in fact be misleading. Applying the formula as a matter of interest, however, might yield some instructive results.

Of the hundreds of persons who have written and taught about God's kingdom, few seem to have attempted consciously to hold together the various tensions bound up with God's reign or in fact even to have acknowledged them. Often the distinctiveness and potency of a particular kingdom theology is precisely its "ec-centricity," its stress on one side only of a polarity (the kingdom as fundamentally *earthly* or fundamentally *heavenly,* for example). In recent decades it has become more generally recognized that whatever the mysteries of the kingdom, it is in key respects both present and future; the "already-but-not-yet" kingdom. Of the examples cited in this book, some obviously maintain the tensions better than others.

It seems to me that E. Stanley Jones's kingdom theology holds in tension the six polarities better than any other example I have encountered. Jones was in fact quite explicit about this both/and way of affirming God's reign. He argued that the kingdom was both inward and outward, both present and future. He stressed both its individual and its social dimensions. He insisted that the kingdom was not the church, and yet he maintained a key linkage between the two:

> Christ loved the Church and gave Himself for it that He might redeem it. But He never gave Himself for the Kingdom to redeem it. For the Kingdom is itself redemption. It is not the subject of redemption—it offers it. The difference is profound. The Church may be, and is, the agent of the coming of that redemption, but it is the agent and not the Absolute. I am bound to be loyal to the Church to the degree that it is loyal to the Kingdom, but my highest loyalty is to the Kingdom, and when these loyalties conflict, then I must bow the knee finally to the Kingdom. Any false loyalty to the Church which would make it take the place of the Kingdom is destructive to the Church.[1]

In Jones's view the kingdom is God's action and design but also has a key place for human action. And its coming may be understood as *both* gradual and cataclysmic. Jesus emphasized both, Jones argued: "Though gripped by the fact of the sudden cataclysmic coming, He did not overlook the quiet, unobtrusive coming of that Kingdom in individual acceptance and in corporate permeation."[2]

Jones also steered between the poles of optimism and pessimism. He was heartily optimistic that the kingdom is the only ultimate realism. But it is often hidden from view, overlooked and ignored by nations, the church, and individual believers. Jones believed the church had largely by-passed or misunderstood the kingdom. Yet, he was convinced of its ultimate triumph.

DISPENSATIONAL MODELS

At the opposite extreme from comprehensive, inclusive models of the kingdom such as Jones's stands dispensationalism. Dispensational models divide God's redemptive activity into separate time periods or "dispensations," often according to some biblical schema (the six days of creation; the biblical covenants; the seven churches of Rev. 2–3). Dispensationalism resolves the inherent tensions in biblical teaching about the kingdom through a process of segmentation. We noted briefly some dispensational views when discussing the kingdom as future hope (model one). Most dispensational constructions in fact fit the Future Kingdom model, though not all. A postmillennial dispensationalism, for example, might fall within the countersystem, transformative, or theocratic model.

Since dispensationalism has at times played a key role in the church and in its relationship to society, it may be useful here to explore it briefly. Some knowledge of dispensationalism is necessary in order for one to comprehend certain popular kingdom theologies, and especially modern premillennialism.[3]

Dispensational views often arise from or employ distinctions based directly or indirectly on Scripture. For example, the kingdom has been understood as:

> Kingdom of God / Kingdom of Heaven
> Kingdom of Israel / Kingdom of Christ
> Kingdom of Law / Kingdom of Grace
> Kingdom of the Father / Kingdom of Christ / Kingdom of the Spirit
> Kingdom of Nature / Kingdom of Grace / Kingdom of Glory

How many kingdoms are there, then? One, two, three, or more? Most writers speak of one kingdom of God, which appears or manifests itself under different aspects. Varying terms highlight different facets of the one kingdom. Or they may refer to the different ways the one kingdom has been manifested in history—for example, Old Covenant, New Covenant, and (in the future or beyond history) New Jerusalem.

Triadic conceptions of the kingdom naturally lend themselves to some correlation with the Persons of the Trinity—spiritually, historically, or both. These trinitarian aspects may then be understood sequentially, concurrently, or as some kind of mystery. The most profound and influential elaboration of such thinking was probably that of Joachim of Fiore.

The fundamental idea of dispensationalism is that God reveals himself differently in different periods in history.[4] Thus a dispensation is "a period of time in which God works with [humankind] in a different way than He does in another period of time."[5] The influential dispensationalist Lewis Sperry Chafer (1871–1952), disciple of C. I. Scofield and founder of Dallas Theological Seminary, explained the dispensational approach as follows: "The Bible may be apportioned into well-defined periods. These periods are clearly separated and the recognition of their divisions with their divine purposes constitutes one of the most important factors in true interpretation of the Scriptures."[6]

Given the many sets of numbers in Scripture, the dispensational approach can yield two, three, seven, or even twelve dispensations. Once one begins to work with such "scriptural arithmetic,"[7] the multiple options permit much flexibility in figuring out God's timetable—enough to make it possible at any point in history to deduce that we are now in the last or next-to-last age and the final climax is just over the next hill.

Dispensational theories may view the kingdom as only one phase in God's plan rather than the overall framework of salvation history.[8] This is the case with modern premillennial dispensationalism. Here the hope of the kingdom is postponed to the millennium after the Second Coming of Christ. Jesus came initially announcing the kingdom; this, however, was rejected by Israel, effectively postponing the kingdom and inaugurating the church age. This line of thought yields, in one of its purest forms, the Future Kingdom model.

In contrast, other forms of dispensationalism may see the kingdom present now, the church representing the Kingdom of Christ. This is the case in Jonathan Edwards's moderate dispensationalism. The kingdom, according to Edwards (1703–1758), is "that evangelical state of things in his church, and in the world, wherein consists the success of Christ's redemption" in the final period of history. "The setting up of the Kingdom of Christ is chiefly accomplished by four successive great events" or dispensations: Christ's appearing in the apostolic age; the "destruction of the heathen Roman empire" under Constantine; the destruction of Antichrist; and "the last judgment, which is the event principally signified in Scripture by Christ's coming in his kingdom." According to Edwards, "Christ's coming in Constantine's time was accompanied with a glorious spiritual resurrection of the greater part of the known world, in a restoration of it to a visible church state from a state of heathenism."[9] Edwards developed these ideas on a postmillennial framework and intimated that the millennial age of the church was beginning to dawn in his own day, in part through the events of the Great Awakening.

A scheme of six or seven "days" as a way of viewing history was employed in the church as early as the first or second century. Many variations of this idea have appeared, not all of them technically dispensational. The scholarly Lactantius (c. 250–c. 325), tutor to one of Emperor Constantine's sons, for example, thought history would run for six thousand years and then be followed by a millennium. In his view the six thousand years would end and the millennium begin around the year 500.[10]

More fully dispensational was the thought of the French Protestant pastor and mystic Pierre Poiret (1646–1719), editor of the works of Madame Guyon. Poiret divided history into six dispensations: the "economies" of Creation, sin, the restoration before the incarnation of Christ, the restoration after the incarnation of Christ, the cooperation of humankind with the operation of God, and universal obedience.[11] Modern premillennial dispensationalism as set forth in the *Scofield Reference Bible* has seven dispensations:

1. Innocence—from creation of Adam and Eve to the Fall
2. Conscience—from the Fall to the Flood
3. Human Government—from the Flood to Abraham
4. Promise—from Abraham to the giving of the Law at Mt. Sinai
5. Law—from Sinai to the close of Jesus' public ministry
6. Grace—from the closing days of Jesus' public ministry
   to the Second Coming
7. Kingdom—the thousand-year reign of Christ on earth.[12]

These examples show how easily millennial and dispensational theories arise when people attempt to understand history in terms of the biblical hope of the kingdom. If the kingdom is promised but not yet here in fullness, one has several options for resolving this already/not yet tension. It can be resolved historically, sacramentally, mystically, psychologically, or dispensationally. Dispensationalism finds its approach most convincing and biblically sound. In the process, however, it runs the risk of dissolving much of the mystery of the kingdom, forcing history into a rigid framework. It may clamp a hermeneutical grid onto Scripture that is as limiting and artificial as, say, doctrinaire Marxism or capitalism, late nineteenth-century liberalism, or modern relativistic humanism. Many people find dispensationalism satisfying, however, precisely because it provides answers—a sense of certainty in a shifting world.

The more basic question, however, is not whether a theory or model provides answers but whether it discloses truth. The two are not necessarily the same.

MODELS AND TRUTH

As suggested in chapter 1, models can be a way either to by-pass questions of truth or to wrestle with them. No particular model, nor all of them together, exhausts the truth that the models seek to express.

In physics, both wave and particle models of light are regarded as expressing truth about the nature of light. It may not be clear whether these models really explain the nature of light or whether, instead, light is fundamentally different from the models in spite of the fact that it is considerate enough to behave in ways that are consistent with them. The models are close enough to the truth that we can use light and harness its power. Thus, informally, we say we know what light "is." This is a "lower order" analogy of the role of models in religious discourse. What appears to be paradox in fact points to a more profound mystery, yet what we perceive as mystery is somehow accessible to our experience.

Consider the phenomenon of religious conversion. Conversion can be and has been analyzed psychologically; it is a sociopsychological phenomenon that is exhibited in many different kinds of conversions: to Christ; to a particular philosophy; to Communism; to atheism. The Christian believes, however, that the truth of conversion to Christ through faith is more than a psychological process, more than merely something inside the mind or spirit of the believer. The psychological model may be true and helpful as far as it goes. But there is that which transcends the model; which it can't capture. The very Spirit of God is somehow at work within the human spirit so that in being "born again" one is truly "born of the Spirit" (John 3:8), not just in one's mind.

This, of course, is a faith affirmation; it cannot be "proved" in a scientific sense or by logical demonstration. Still, the logic of the argument is clear: Being born of the Spirit by definition transcends our minds, our logical categories and powers. Logic and intuition tell us that conversion to Christ must transcend our logical explanations and models, whether they be those of psychology, philosophy, sociobiology, or for that matter theology, if God transcends our individual and collective human existence.[13] So we must fall back on models like physical birth (John 3) or physical resurrection (Eph. 2) or the healing of disease (Isa. 53:5), using these to express a spiritual reality that is analogous to these experiences and yet is also fundamentally different—as different as the difference between flesh and spirit (John 1:13; 3:6).

So it is with models of the kingdom. They clarify; they may oversimplify and also overly complicate or even confuse; and ultimately they leave us still with the question of *faith*—what we believe about God and the ways that Jesus Christ is revealed to us individually and in community.[14]

Is there, then, any way of mediating among the models? Do we simply adopt those that feel right or seem most persuasive? Is there any test for truth? I believe there are at least three fundamental tests for truth in examining models of the kingdom, some of which have already been implied in foregoing chapters.

Avery Dulles, in *Models of the Church,* suggests seven criteria for evaluating ecclesiological models: (1) their basis in Scripture, (2) their basis in the Christian tradition, (3) their capacity to give church members a sense of their corporate identity and mission, (4) their tendency to foster the virtues and values generally admired by Christians, (5) their correspondence with people's religious experience today, (6) their theological fruitfulness, and (7) their fruitfulness in enabling church members to relate successfully to those outside their own group. Dulles notes, "One criterion for the selection of new paradigms is their ability to solve problems that proved intractable by appeal to the older models, or to synthesize doctrines that previously appeared to be unrelated." With John Stuart Mill and H. Richard Niebuhr he argues that people "are more apt to be correct in what they affirm than in what they deny."[15] As Niebuhr wrote in *Christ and Culture,* "What we deny is generally something that lies outside our experience, and about which we can therefore say nothing."[16]

These criteria are useful also in assessing models of the kingdom. I would focus, however, specifically on the three following criteria.

1. For the Christian, the first test must be fidelity to the Word of God—above all fidelity to Jesus Christ, the Living Word, and then to the Scriptures, which testify of Christ. In part this is a question of maintaining the several biblical tensions or polarities discussed in chapter 1. This is a conceptual, theological task. It means examining any conception of God's reign in the light of the tensions between present and future, earth and heaven, and so on. It is also an existential task, however. Can the tensions be maintained not just in theory but in the nitty-gritty daily life of Christian community and Christian living in the world?

The more fundamental issue here, however, is fidelity to the person and spirit of Jesus Christ as revealed to us in the Bible. Despite all the complicated hermeneutical questions that arise when we attempt to interpret Scripture, a clear and consistent picture of Jesus the Messiah emerges from the New Testament when we approach the Scriptures humbly, continuously, prayerfully and with openness to the Spirit, and within Christian community. The picture of Jesus emerges more clearly from Scripture than does the profile of the kingdom. Therefore, the kingdom of God is to be interpreted in the light of Jesus Christ. It then becomes true as well that Jesus Christ is to be understood in the light of biblical kingdom themes.

Both theologically and experientially, Jesus embodies in his person all the kingdom polarities we have delineated. The more Christocentric, in a biblical sense, our understanding of the kingdom, the more likely it is to approximate the truth.

Part of the issue here is the fundamental hermeneutical question of the relationship between the Old and New Testaments. As all Scripture is to be interpreted in the light of Jesus Christ, so the Old Testament is to be interpreted in the light of the New. Failure to follow this principle yields a kingdom more of law than of grace, as we noted particularly in discussing the Theocratic Kingdom.

But a necessary caution is in order here. The New Testament does not simply "spiritualize" the Old; nor is the moral law as revealed in the Old Testament abolished in its fulfillment in Jesus Christ (Matt. 5:17). This is especially important in discussing the issue of God's reign. The transition from Old Covenant to New Covenant is not a pendulum swing from the earthly to the heavenly, from the present to the future, or from society or nation to the individual. Rather, in Jesus Christ all the earthly, this-worldly promises of the kingdom find and will find their *fulfillment* according to the reality of both the incarnation and the resurrection of Jesus Christ. The biblical doctrine of the kingdom shows that God intends to save humankind *with* their environment, not *out of* it.[17]

2. A second key test regarding kingdom models concerns the corporate life of Christians in the church. This relates to Dulles's third and fourth criteria. Does a given model of the kingdom help generate and maintain a vital Christian community of worship, witness, and mutual interdependence, or does it undermine it? Like the church, the kingdom is a social reality, not merely a private hope or a mental theory. Biblically faithful models of God's reign nurture and enrich the church's shared life together. Churches that vitally embody the gospel are churches with an active kingdom vision.

3. Does one's model of the kingdom inspire and nurture redemptive Christian living in the world? This is the third test. Jesus' being in the world meant truly being *in* the world—in the streets, in the marketplace, with the sick and troubled, and in the homes of the despised. So it is with the church. The most faithful and useful models of the kingdom are those that undergird the church's mission in the world, prompting both an immediacy of witness and action and a certain calm patience based in the confidence that the kingdom is fundamentally God's work, not ours. We confess that our present efforts, successful or unsuccessful as they may be, point ahead and contribute to a more ultimate reconciliation whose final coming is not in doubt.

MODELS, TRUTH, AND LOVE

God is love, and though no one has ever seen God, we do see God's love in Jesus Christ. Jesus is love as God is love. And yet Jesus is also the truth (John 1:14-18, 14:6-10; I John 4:7-12). Are these two ways of saying the same thing? The issue is important today in looking at the nature of Jesus and the kingdom because of the modern tendency in many churches to say in effect: It doesn't matter what you believe as long as you act in love.

Scripture holds together love and truth as aspects of God's nature and self-revelation. God is truth; God is love. And the church is to be the messianic community that "speaks the truth in love." But existentially there is often a tension here: Love is so elevated that questions of truth become fuzzy, or (more typically in conservative circles) truth is so stressed that love is sacrificed. This is a key tension and a key theological issue that to some degree shapes how we evaluate the various models of the kingdom.

At this point four differing perspectives seem to operate in the church:

1. Love is more important than truth. Truth is elusive and uncertain and, in any case, highly subjective, but we know what love is. To raise the question of truth is to sidetrack us from ethics into doctrine. If we concentrate on love, truth will take care of itself. Often utopian visions of the kingdom tend in this direction.

2. Truth is more important than love. This is fundamentalism in its various forms. Love is important, but easily degenerates into permissiveness or relativism or "sloppy agape." In the name of love we may sacrifice truth, ultimately losing the doctrinal base upon which true love must be built. Some versions of the kingdom in history have demonstrated this tendency.

3. Truth is love, and love is truth. Since both truth and love express God's nature, there can be no conflict between the two. Love, and you will be led into truth; if you want to know the truth, love. Love is not more important than truth, but the two are part of the same whole, so true love will lead to real truth. The greatest defining truth is love.

There is a better way of formulating the issue, however, a way that is more faithful to Scripture. This would be the fourth position:

4. Truth and love are bound together and united in a higher reality. There is something greater and higher than either truth or love, and that something is in fact Some One—the triune, personal God revealed in Scripture and supremely in Jesus Christ. This is the God who says:

> I live in a high and holy place,
> but also with [whoever] is contrite and
> lowly in spirit. (Isa. 57:15)

Here we see God as both transcendent and immanent. Thus love and truth are not abstract principles or forces; they are ways of speaking of God and how God has revealed himself to us. It is in Jesus Christ that we find both truth and love; Jesus is "the way, the truth, and the life" and the perfect manifestation of the love of God. His whole life and work are the model for Christian existence (Phil. 2:4-13) and fundamentally reveal the character of the kingdom of God.

This affirmation carries with it the corollary that we may compromise the love of God either by insisting on "truth" in a way that becomes unloving or by so emphasizing love—the love of God or of Jesus—that we undercut the *truth basis* for love.

At stake here fundamentally is the question of the character of God. God is portrayed in Scripture as a Person of moral character. Biblically the word for God's character is *holiness,* that fiery, loving passion that necessarily reveals itself as both tenderness and judgment and that teaches us that love involves not only forgiveness but also accountability.

This presents a high challenge to the church as it seeks to live in the light of God's reign. The church is to affirm and embody both the truth and the love of God. In fact, the greatest challenge, in the light of all the issues raised by God's kingdom, is this: how to be authentically Christian in our present environment; how to lead the kind of life that gives credibility to the theology we affirm. The kingdom, like Jesus, is grounded in both truth and love. So the church must undergird its theology with Christlike living. Otherwise it loses its credibility.

The various models of the kingdom need to be examined from this perspective. In the light of the character of God as revealed in Jesus Christ, God incarnate, we see that no one model is fully adequate, some are more useful than others, and some are incompatible with the gospel. As Dulles wrote regarding models of the church, "Although all the models have their merits, they are not of equal worth, and some presentations of some models must positively be rejected."[18] It is also sometimes true that a model itself and the way it is fleshed out in the church may be two quite different things.

Of the eight models we have examined, the kingdom as institutional church, as political state, and as earthly utopia seem least to fit the criteria suggested in this chapter. The other five models accent key elements of biblical teaching about God's reign, none of which can be lost without impoverishing the church's inner life or its outward witness. Though historical context or other factors may bring one or another of these models to the fore at different times, none should be totally overlooked.

What does it mean concretely for the church to embody and reflect truthfully and lovingly the reality of the kingdom today, both globally and locally? These are the key questions underlying the final two chapters of this book.

11 THE GOSPEL OF THE KINGDOM AND THE GLOBAL ECONOMY

WHAT DOES our journey through the past and present understandings of God's reign say about the future? This question increasingly presses as the world becomes one global society. In this chapter we will explore some issues raised by the church's emerging global context and suggest two themes that can help to "globalize" our kingdom models: ecological interdependence and the metaphor of cosmic drama.

When the Christian faith burst the wineskins of Judaism and spread throughout the Greco-Roman world, it faced in new ways the question of universal history. First- and second-century Christians came to see Jesus not only as promised Messiah but also as the Christ of history and of the cosmos.

The New Testament writers who most engaged the Greco-Roman mind spoke of the Logos who became flesh, of Jesus Christ who upholds "all things by his powerful word" (Heb. 1:3), and as the one through whom God was reconciling and bringing together in the fullness of time all things in heaven and on earth, visible and invisible (see Col. 1:16-20). Part of the unique power of the gospel was its universal cosmic message in an age when universal, cosmic questions were being asked. Through concepts such as "economy" (*oikonomia*), Logos, "mystery," and kingdom, Christian thinkers of the first two centuries articulated with varying success a universal message grounded in the particularity of the birth, life, death, and resurrection of Jesus Christ.

A similar task faces the church today.

"Kingdom of God" is one of the primary symbols by which the church has maintained and explained this universal character of the gospel message. The need to stress this universality of the gospel has, however, varied considerably down through history. Times of discovery of "new worlds" inevitably push this question to the fore, requiring the church to state anew its faith that the good news of Jesus Christ is for all times and places and peoples. The first century was such a time. So were the fifteenth and sixteenth centuries and, increasingly, the modern period since the eighteenth century. Christians have found varying ways to articulate the universality of the Christian message as the times and the questions have shifted.

Our world is becoming one in ways that were never before true in history. Whether one looks at politics and economics, transportation and communications, science and technology, or entertainment and the arts, the picture is the same: convergence, internationalization, interdependence, global competition. Ours is a time of new models and paradigms as never before. This constitutes perhaps the greatest theological challenge for the church since the first century.

The discussion of models of the kingdom should be set within this context. What does the examination of various models of the kingdom say about the church's mission in a new global economy? Is there a new or renewed kingdom theology for the new millennium? Are there new models that may be useful?

The church will need a universal or "cosmic" theology that will engage the mind (or minds) of the age without compromising the truth of Jesus Christ or biblical revelation. This is true both in areas of the world where the church has "grown old" and in areas of effective evangelization and rapid church growth. In these newer churches the second and third generations of believers will be asking similar universal questions, even if their parents didn't.

Whether such a theology is articulated in terms of "kingdom of God" or through some other models or metaphors, it will need to pass the two tests of contemporary relevance and biblical fidelity. Beyond that, it seems to me that a theology with universal appeal must be marked by at least six characteristics.

1. It will give a plausible explanation of the relationship between spirit and matter, providing a convincing account of the spiritual dimensions of existence.

2. It will provide a theology of the environment, not as a secondary concern but as part of a fundamental ecological orientation that affirms and explains the interrelationship between all things in the present and over the course of time.

3. It will be economic in the sense of providing an overall framework for affirming and understanding economics, politics, and social interaction generally.

4. It will articulate a theology of Christian experience that meets deep, personal human needs and yet is engaged with society and a global perspective.

5. It will have a strong theology of the church that joins the local congregation of worship, community, and witness organically with history and with God's overall plan "for the fullness of time, to gather up all things on

earth [in Jesus Christ]" (Eph. 1:10 NRSV). This, of course, is again the question of the relationship between the church and the kingdom.

6. A relevant kingdom theology for the twenty-first century will affirm a God who is distinct from and yet intimately involved with every aspect of the universe—a God who is both love and truth, a God of sovereign power and yet of ultimate compassion and self-giving. It will affirm Jesus Christ as fully human and fully God, perhaps finding new formulations for this traditional affirmation. This means seeing Jesus Christ as the cosmic Christ and the personal Christ, as redeemer and liberator, the one in whom both our personal and social lives and all of history find their ultimate meaning.

Although these issues may be new in the way they come to us now, Scripture addresses them profoundly. From the Old Testament prophets to Jesus' own words; from the promise of creation and the covenant with Noah and Abraham and all Israel to the vision of cosmic reconciliation in the book of Revelation, Scripture speaks of a gospel that is universal and ultimate. The challenge to the church worldwide as we enter a new millennium will be to articulate the "eternal gospel" (Rev. 14:6) with freshness, creativity, and power once again.

If we are indeed entering today the age of geoeconomics rather than the age of geopolitics,[1] this will force Christians globally to rethink the nature of God's kingdom. In fact, this seems to be happening already. *Can* the kingdom of God be usefully conceived of in a geoeconomic way? May this suggest new dimensions to ancient Greek and Christian conceptions of "economy"?[2]

TRENDS AND CHALLENGES

The church has always considered itself "universal." But today this is empirically true as never before. In the nineteen centuries following the resurrection of Jesus, Christianity grew to embrace one-third of all humanity; yet, more than 80 percent of these were white. In the twentieth century Christianity has become a global faith, the most universal religion in history. The church is growing rapidly in many of the populous, poorer nations of the southern hemisphere. Today Christians number about one-third of all humanity and more than half the population in two-thirds of the world's 223 nations. The Christian church has become an amalgam of the world's races and peoples, with whites dropping from over 80 percent to about 40 percent. This is the global reality, but it is not the way most North American Christians and theologians, often mired in stagnant churches, see the picture.

This new internationalization of the church is producing a historic revolution: a shift of the church's "center of gravity" from the North and West (mainly Europe and North America) to the Two-Thirds World. In 1900 the northern hemisphere counted some 462 million Christians, 83 percent of the world total, while the South had about 96 million Christians, or 17 percent of the total. By 1980 the church in the South had grown to 700 million, nearly half of the world total. Today the church of the historically "Christian" nations is probably the minority church worldwide.[3]

Missiologist Walbert Bühlmann puts this change in perspective: "What is effectively the centre of gravity of Christianity in the West has shifted more and more," reaching the critical point in 1970 where 51 percent of Roman Catholics were living in the southern continents of Latin America, Africa, and Asia-Oceania. "By the year 2000 a good 70 percent of all Catholics will be living in the southern hemisphere," he notes. This is similar to trends for the whole Christian church.

Bühlmann points out the significance of this shift:

> The Third Church is approaching, church of the Third World but also church of the third millennium. Roughly speaking we can say that the first Christian millennium, with the first eight councils all held in the East, stood mainly under the leadership of the First Church, the Eastern church; the second millennium stood under the leadership of the Second Church, the Western church, which shaped the Middle Ages. . . . Now the coming third millennium will evidently stand under the leadership of the Third Church, the Southern church. I am convinced that the most important drives and inspirations for the whole church in the future will come from the Third Church.[4]

What do these changes mean for the future? We shall likely see a World Church emerge that is much more diverse ethnically and culturally; exhibits a greater mutual respect for the leadership, styles, ministries, and traditions of other Christian believers; is increasingly urban; and ministers more intentionally to the poor, oppressed, and suffering.

With the world becoming one interconnected global communications network, the unprecedented Christian growth worldwide is bound to affect the traditionally Christian lands of North America and Europe. In the twenty-first century the main currents of influence in the World Church will flow from Third World areas to Europe and North America, reversing a three hundred-year trend. To a significant degree the same will be true ideologically and politically beyond the church as the debtor status of the United States eventually undercuts its political and economic dominance in the world.

Pressures for a new "world theology" that expands the way Christians understand the universe and their role in it will come from economic, social, scientific, and political developments now shaping the world. These range from world health and environmental concerns to increasing economic interdependency to concerns over nuclear weapons. Additionally, the next twenty years will likely see a major breakthrough in scientific understanding of the fundamental nature of the physical universe. Since Einstein's theory of relativity was published in 1915 scientists have been seeking a general Theory of Everything (TOE) or Grand Unified Theory (GUT) that would link the four basic forces of nature: gravity, electromagnetism, and the strong and weak forces of nuclear energy.

Scientific discovery and verification of a unified theory of the physical universe would have profound theological and practical implications. It would be a new Copernican revolution. This underscores the need for a plausible Christian theology of the universe—a convincing "Christian Theory of Everything" that is both biblically sound and scientifically believable. This is a challenge much like the one second- and third-century Christian apologists faced.

ECOLOGY AND THE KINGDOM OF GOD

As economic integration and ecological awareness grow worldwide, Christians will increasingly think in ecological terms and will begin to apply the model of ecology to the church's life and thought. A theology of the kingdom will have to embrace and account for economic and ecological realities and perspectives.[5]

To think ecologically need not mean moving away from Scripture. The Bible in fact is fundamentally ecological in perspective. We see this in six ways:

1. Both ecology and the Bible view the world in a long-range time frame. Human beings are accustomed to measuring time in terms of a life span, at most. We have a short-range view. Most human planning reaches only a few years or decades ahead. But to understand ecological reality, we must speak of hundreds or thousands of years. Ecological problems, for example, may be many generations in building and can seldom be solved in a few years' time.

The biblical perspective is ecologically long-range. The Bible itself was written over a period of many centuries. It traces history back to creation and makes the connections straight through from Adam and Eve to Jesus Christ and on to the final culmination of the kingdom of God. Each human life is seen as important and as fitting into God's long-range purposes in history.

2. Both ecology and the Bible see the natural world as one interconnected whole. This, of course, is the point of the ecological perspective. Here the doctrine of creation is central. Everything is interrelated because all comes from the hand of God and finds meaning in God's purposes. God creates

matter, and the human form is fashioned from the dust of the earth. Each form of life reproduces "after its kind" and is related to the rest of creation. Even the heavenly bodies come from the hand of God. From this perspective the Bible is profoundly ecological.

Ecology speaks of the web of life, of diversity and mutuality, of dynamism and change. In the Bible life's interdependent web is pictured historically in many of the narrative sections of Scripture and poetically in Job and many of the psalms. A large number of the psalms are really creation hymns, glorying not in an abstract God but in the divine wisdom, power, and care displayed in the intricate ordering of the natural environment.

3. Both ecology and the Bible focus on the significance of land. Man and woman do not live independently of the land. They are linked to the land and exploit or ruin it at their peril.

Walter Brueggemann underscores this point in his book *The Land*. The Bible is not, Brueggemann argues, the story of God and God's people only, but of God, God's people, and the land. Land, both as "actual earthly turf" and as symbol of rootedness or "historical belonging," Brueggemann believes, is "a central [theme] . . . of biblical faith." Keeping the biblical focus on land before us "will protect us from excessive spiritualization, so that we recognize that the yearning for land is always a serious historical enterprise concerned with historical power and belonging."[6]

We recall here the many biblical promises concerning land, beginning especially with the covenant with Abraham (Gen. 12:7; 17:8). The biblical emphasis on the land is particularly striking from an ecological standpoint. In both Scripture and ecology, the ideal is man and woman living at home on the land in an environment of balance, harmony, and mutual dependence. It is neither biblically nor ecologically sound to view humanity as living independently from the land. And it is fundamentally unecological and ultimately suicidal, both spiritually and physically, to attempt autonomous life divorced or alienated from the land.

4. Both ecology and the Bible present us with an awareness of limits.[7] This a hard fact, a stubborn ecological reality. Our ecosphere is limited in its matter and energy. Even solar power is limited, both absolutely and in the degree to which it can be captured on earth. Resources that appeared limitless to an expanding frontier population now are seen to be finite as population bulges into the billions.

Scripture underscores this reality of limits. At creation God separated the light from the darkness (Gen. 1:4) and established the limits of earth and sea (Gen. 1:9). Creation itself may be viewed as a process of separating and setting limits. The psalmist says that God "set the boundaries of the earth" and "made both summer and winter" (Ps. 74:17).

Man and woman are limited because of their physical existence, even though created in the image of God. And God marks off moral limits for humanity, initially (Gen. 2:15-16), after the Fall (Gen. 3:16-19), and on down through the course of salvation history and the formation of a special people of God. God provides structures and boundaries for the well-being of his creation. This is limitation for the sake of further growth—a deeply ecological concept, as every gardener knows.

God is forever saying to man and woman, in effect: "Here are the limits. Abide by them according to my purposes, and you will live. Spurn them and you will die." Ecologically viewed, such limitation is neither arbitrary nor exclusively spiritual. It is physical as well because of the nature of the material world God has given us. God and the world of spirit are limitless and are the realities through which we transcend the limits of space and time. But as physical creatures human beings live within limits to which they must adapt.

5. Both ecology and the Bible see the natural order as subject to decay. Plants and animals die; hills erode; species become extinct. Ecologically, we face here not just the transitoriness of nature but the fact of entropy, the second law of thermodynamics. Entropy is a measure of disorder in a system. According to the law of entropy, the disorder in our universe is increasing as more and more resources are transformed from usable to unusable form.

Physicists tell us that even the most efficient machines produce some waste, and the energy lost as waste can never be fully recovered. Thus available energy is always decreasing; waste (as various forms of pollution) is always increasing; and overall the universe is moving from order to disorder as more and more matter and energy are turned into waste products. This process has become critical in our age because of the awesome power of technology to speed it up.

Scripture gives us a similar picture. We read that "the creation was subjected to frustration, not by its own choice, but by the will of the one who subjected it, in hope that the creation itself will be liberated from its bondage to decay and brought into the glorious freedom of the children of God" (Rom. 8:20-21). The natural world is not a perfectly balanced, self-sustaining machine. Human sin and rebellion have had their negative impact on the natural order. While we may not know the precise ways sin affects our world, nature is in some fundamental sense disordered because of the Fall. Like human nature itself, the physical world suffers not only from human sin but also from some more basic derangement, some "bondage to decay." This is reflected in part in the curse pronounced after the Fall (Gen. 3:17-19). Like humankind, the earth still shows forth the glory of its maker but in a defaced, partially ruined way.

6. Both ecology and the Bible show that all behavior has consequences. Ecologically speaking, we can never say that anything we do simply doesn't matter. The effect of one person's life may be minimal, but it does have environmental impact—physically, socially, economically, and spiritually. Every breath breathed, every dollar spent, and every relationship created modifies the universe. We are tempted to think one person's impact is so small as to be irrelevant, but that is a profoundly antiecological attitude. Our new environmental awareness shows us that when added to the experience of hundreds of millions of others, every person's behavior is ecologically significant *in all its dimensions.*

Ecology tells us to watch out especially for long-range consequences. Our behavior touches not only the present world but all future generations. Whether we are speaking about biology (for instance, the creation of families), economics (for instance, the accumulation of wealth) or technology (for instance, the production of radioactive wastes), our behavior as humans makes ripples that radiate ahead into future generations. Thus even from a purely ecological perspective we can say that ethical questions are an inevitable part of life on earth.

In all these respects, the biblical worldview is profoundly ecological. All behavior has meaning and consequences because of who God is and because of the nature of the physical-spiritual universe in which God has placed us. We are faced again with the reality, "Do this, and you will live; do that, and you will die." We have tended to think of such consequences as arbitrary fiats of God. God has set the rules, and, for his own sovereign and inscrutable reasons, if we break the rules we get zapped. But the ecological perspective points to a much deeper truth: We suffer the consequences of our actions because of the nature of the physical, spiritual, moral universe God has created—which reflects, of course, the very character of God.

The rule is, "The soul who sins is the one who will die" (Ezek. 18:4). But this is not really a rule; it is the nature of the case, part of the spiritual ecology of God's world. All behavior has consequences, those consequences are often long-range, and ethical questions are inescapable.

In all these ways, then, ecological and biblical perspectives are similar. From the viewpoint of Christian faith, this is not surprising. The closer ecological science comes to the real nature of things, the closer it will approach the biblical picture.

The universe is ordered not logically, psychologically, or sociologically, but ecologically. The ecological perspective affirms and encompasses all other dimensions. Both the Bible and ecology show man and woman living interdependently with the natural environment. Ideally the relationship between humanity and our environment is *symbiotic*—a mutually supportive, interdependent living *with*—rather than parasitic. But in our disordered world, man and woman have become parasites on the environment. Both ecological and spiritual health require understanding the necessary interdependence of humankind and the natural environment, and of taking both ecology and Scripture seriously.

Scripture, however, claims a fundamental priority over ecology because it reveals what ecology can never fully explain: the realm of the spirit, the dimension of spiritual reality. According to the Bible, we do not really understand the ecology of the world until we recognize its source, the Lord God, and that the space-time physical world is interpenetrated and held together by a spiritual world and by spiritual energy that comes from God. From this standpoint, we really are not thinking ecologically—even from a scientific point of view—if we do not include the dimension of the spirit.

The Bible pictures both the church and the kingdom in fundamentally ecological ways. It presents the church through what might be called ecological word pictures: body, family, vine, and branches. The biblical conception of God's reign is also an ecological conception. The fruit of God's unhindered rule is *shalom*—a life of harmony, health and peace. Biblical *shalom* is very close to the concept of ecological balance so far as its implications for nature are concerned—though, of course, *shalom* is much more than this because it includes righteousness and justice and the full restoration of the image of God in human life and community.

ECOLOGY AND KINGDOM ECONOMICS

God's plan is God's *oikonomia,* his economy for the fullness of time. The economy of God is the "plan" of the kingdom of God. It is the reconciling and uniting of all things, visible and invisible, under the authority of Jesus Christ. This plan is both ecological and economic; both ecology and economics concern the "household" (*oikos*). While this is not the place to discuss economic questions thoroughly, we should note several points that must be a part of kingdom economics.

God is the owner of everything, including all resources and the means of production. God owns both land and capital, which human beings hold in trust for God's glory and the common good. This places serious limitations on private ownership of resources and on the private accumulation of wealth.

Kingdom economics will challenge both capitalist and socialist ideology, seeking new economic options that incorporate the valid elements of various systems. Economics must recognize the finiteness and vulnerability of our ecosystem and the seriousness of environmental issues, seeking to preserve and protect earth's biosphere. It must recognize the genius of human community as a key factor in economic policy and organization. This means, among other things, working to support and encourage human-scale economic arrangements that build neighborhoods, local communities, and families.

Given the vulnerability of the biosphere, the limits of resources, and the nature of human community, economics must focus on small- and intermediate-scale organization and technology, not so predominantly on large-scale capital- and energy-intensive technology and organization as has been the case for the past century. Finally, economics must give special attention to the poor and oppressed, recognizing that every person has moral, ecological, and economic significance and that all our lives are interdependent. Kingdom economics will demonstrate that, when the full ecology of our world is understood, caring for the poor and oppressed is actually economic wisdom as well as moral sense.

God's kingdom plan is in part a matter of economics. The kingdom of God does point in some specific economic directions, even if it does not give us a full economic theory. In this perspective the significance of seeing the kingdom as God's economy and ecology emerges with special force.

These considerations suggest additional perspectives for assessing the eight kingdom models examined in the foregoing chapters and evaluating their relevance for today. We can ask about their economic and ecological impact in the fullest sense of these terms. It might be possible in fact to trace the outlines of a "new," or at least refined, model of the kingdom from this angle—the kingdom as God's ecology-economy.

But let us move finally to more poetic ways of envisioning God's reign.

THE KINGDOM AS COSMIC DRAMA

Global awareness and ecological realities make us increasingly conscious of larger, more cosmic dimensions of human existence. In the light of this, we might look in another direction as we seek to comprehend God's redemptive purpose and activity. A quite different way of addressing the issues involved with kingdom theologies would be to imagine God's plan as a cosmic drama.

In this view, God is the great Playwright, working out a dramatic plan on the stage of history. God is sovereign as the playwright is sovereign over the drama he or she creates. Yet, as every artist knows, in the creative process sovereignty does not mean lack of engagement, emotional detachment, or total independence from the persons and the action in the play. The playwright feels personally involved with the characters; putting something of herself or himself in them. In fact, each character probably embodies some aspect of the playwright's own character.

In this model the kingdom of God is the great drama of redemption—personal, social, and cosmic. Everything is included; all things in heaven and on earth, visible and invisible. But there is a central story. We see movement, climax, final resolution. While the play is unfolding, only the Playwright sees this fully. For the Christian actor in the midst of the story, meaning and ultimate purpose can be affirmed only by faith—concerning the character of God, the nature of the drama, and the final outcome.

But, some might object, a drama isn't "real" or "true"; it remains a work of fiction, however much truth it embodies or reveals. Most people don't want to see themselves as the projection of someone else's fantasy, as someone's dream—much less as merely playing a part that is already written, the story predetermined.

The drama model, however, allows for this—if we remember that the model is a metaphor for a mystery that transcends the model. In this case the Dramatist really allows the characters to come alive, to improvise, to make real decisions, even possibly to ruin the play or steal the show! The question then becomes not so much the *power* of the Playwright (who can call a halt at will if things get out of hand) but rather the Playwright's intelligence, creativity, and insight—in short, God's *creative genius.* Humanly speaking, the greatest dramatic genius who ever lived could not allow full freedom to the actors on the stage and still be sure the story would turn out as intended, even if the playwright knew all the actors intimately. But if the Playwright were *God*—not a God who predetermines people's actions but a God who gives people genuine freedom within the limits of his ultimate sovereign power—the story would be different. Genuinely contingent, and yet definitely glorious in final outcome. It would be a breathtaking story!

C. S. Lewis's conception of "myth become fact" may be helpful at this point. Lewis recognized that great myths express truth in some sense. The uniqueness of Jesus Christ, however, is that in him the myth of redemption became historical reality. "The heart of Christianity is a myth which is also a fact," Lewis wrote. He suggested that someone who doubted the historical factuality of Jesus Christ "but continually fed on it as myth would, perhaps, be more spiritually alive than one who assented and did not think much about it." But the story of Jesus Christ brings myth and fact together: "Perfect Myth and Perfect Fact: claiming not only our love and our obedience, but also our wonder and delight, addressed to the savage, the child, and the poet in each one of us no less than to the moralist, the scholar, and the philosopher."[8]

From this perspective, all the dramas and myths of humanity testify to a more profound truth: a story of redemption that is both poetry and history. Truth, in the final analysis, must be just so: A beautiful story in which evil is finally overcome (or self-destructs) and in the end we see the harmony, the symmetry. The model of God's redemptive activity as cosmic drama hints at how such a story might just be true—not only poetically or mythically but also historically.

This model has the advantage of being able to maintain the tension of the biblical-kingdom polarities. The story of redemption is *present* in the ongoing drama we experience. The culmination lies in the future; yet, the future is incipiently present now, and those who are in on the secret shape their behavior according to their "insight into the mystery" (Eph. 3:4) of the drama. Clearly the drama is individual and social; drama powerfully captures the interplay between character and social milieu. The distinction between church and kingdom is the distinction between the key actors and the play itself: distinct, yet clearly related. The tension between the kingdom's coming gradually or cataclysmically is easily handled, for any good story includes both gradual development and climactic moments leading to final resolution. So also with the tension between divine and human action. Clearly divine action is primary—initially, finally, and throughout. And yet human action can be conceived of as real, free, and significant. It actually contributes something to the final outcome. There is room for many subplots, counterplots, even attempts to subvert the story. Actors may be tempted to think they are autonomous, or deny that there is any meaning. But the drama unfolds and finally reveals meaning.

Perhaps the most problematic polarity is that between the earthly and the heavenly; matter and spirit. A *deus ex machina* model won't do. But one can imagine a cosmic drama happening in more than one dimension of reality. This is in fact how a number of biblical passages view the drama; it is fundamentally the biblical worldview. In our age C. S. Lewis was a master of this multidimensionality, making multiple levels of reality believable, as for example in the *Perelandra* trilogy and *The Chronicles of Narnia*.[9]

The Christian drama of redemption, in short, can be conceived as happening in several dimensions of reality, yet unified in the being and mind of God. Also, good drama is capable of revealing not only outer behavior but interior reality as well. The conception of God's involvement with human existence as a cosmic drama thus has several strengths. Additional advantages to this model are its compatibility with Scripture as the history and story of God's dealings with humankind, its relevance to both personal and environmental concerns, and its capability of being explored through a variety of forms and symbols. Its corresponding weaknesses must also be acknowledged, and, as with all models, it must be seen as an only partial representation of deeper and broader truth: a model pointing toward, but not exhausting, the mystery.[10]

A theology or model of the kingdom is useful to the degree that it provides guidance for the actual life of the Christian community. It is crucially important that the church think clearly about the kingdom today in the light of the challenges we have noted in this chapter. On the other hand, the place where the rubber meets the road (or better, where the toe meets the turf) is the shared life of the community of Jesus' disciples. We now turn to this matter to conclude our discussion.

12 BUILDING KINGDOM COMMUNITIES TODAY

CHRISTIANS HAVE the audacious hope and make the bold claim that they are building the future in the present. They claim this not merely in the historical sense that today is always becoming tomorrow but in the eschatological sense as well. Our life today as followers of Jesus Christ points toward and in some way brings near the ultimate end and goal of history, the time when God will "restore everything, as he promised long ago through his holy prophets" (Acts 3:21). The discussion in previous chapters has made clear that how boldly or firmly Christians make this claim, and just what they mean by it, can range widely over a broad spectrum.

What do this Christian hope and claim mean for everyday life in the Christian community? The "little flock" of Jesus' disciples can live in confidence because Jesus has promised it "the kingdom" (Luke 12:32). But today the church is not a little flock. It has now become an international community, existing, among other forms, in dozens of ecclesiastical multinational corporations. Can it live in faithfulness to the kingdom it claims?

If God's kingdom is at one and the same time present and future, individual and social, earthly and heavenly, then this gives the church a unique character. A biblical ecclesiology, like a biblical kingdom theology, must maintain the tension of the six polarities regarding the kingdom that are found in Scripture. Part of the wonder of the church is that it exists precisely at the critical intersection between present and future and between earth and heaven.

These are not merely abstract ideas. Rather, they concern practical aspects of the church's life. They have direct implications for the church's worship, community life, and witness.

This is most dramatically clear in the church's worship life. In worship, believers celebrate and experience the present reality of the kingdom in their fellowship with one another and with God in Christ through the presence of the Holy Spirit. Part of the joy and wonder of that experience, however, is precisely the awareness that what we now experience is but a foretaste, an "earnest," of a reality that is promised and is sure to come in

145

fullness because of what God has done decisively in Jesus Christ. In vital worship believers really experience now the presence of God among them. They find their hope for the full coming of the kingdom kindled and reinforced as they worship God together. Worship in fact should be planned and experienced in such a way that these present and future aspects of the kingdom are a part of each worship gathering.

Because the kingdom of God is both individual and social, vital worship provides occasions for believers to sense God's presence with them in their inmost being as well as in community. As heavenly and earthly, worship focuses both on ultimate spiritual realities and on our day-by-day life in the world. Thus the needs and challenges of society are directly the concern of the church as God's messianic servant community. Vital worship has a way of uniting these dimensions so that they reinforce each other rather than leading us off in opposite directions or creating a sort of spiritual schizophrenia.

The same thing holds in regard to the other polarities that make up the reality of the kingdom. Part of the joy and wonder of worship is the awareness that though we are weak and unable to bring about God's kingdom in our own strength, "our God will fight for us" (Neh. 4:20). Worship celebrates God's power and promised victory; it is much more than a religious pep rally to get us ready for our weekly struggle with the world. On the other hand, this celebration of present and coming victory does in fact encourage and equip us so that we can effectively be salt and light in the world rather than an irrelevant religious ghetto. The awareness that this "little flock" of believers is not the kingdom but has received and will inherit the kingdom is a stimulus toward humility and servanthood on the one hand, but also to confidence and courage on the other.

What has been said here about worship applies as well to the church's internal community life and to its witness in the world. Both are to be shaped by the "already but not yet" of the kingdom; by the heavenly and earthly, earthy dimensions; by the wonder of a sovereign God working through responsible disciples. A church conscious of the kingdom will build cohesive community centered in Christ and will do the work of the kingdom in the world.

THE PRACTICAL MEANING OF THE KINGDOM

Throughout this book we have seen the wide variety of meanings that have grown up around the concept of "kingdom of God." Yet, the kingdom is, above all, the good news that Jesus embodied and proclaimed. It is above all the message of Scripture, not the ponderings of theologians. It concerns the way Christians live their daily lives.

What, then, is the kingdom from the standpoint of the "little flock" of believers to whom Jesus promised it? We may summarize the biblical teachings as follows:

1. *The kingdom is God's reign over all,* not so much as a *realm* but as God's continuing sovereign authority and activity over "all things," things in heaven and on earth, visible and invisible; things present and things to come. Thus the affirmation of the kingdom of God is an affirmation that God is not merely Creator, and is not some impersonal, blind force in the universe, but is the God of Scripture who continues to be active in the world.

In this sense, the kingdom always *is*. It is reality; the way things are as well as the way they *will* be. E. Stanley Jones was right, therefore, to say that the kingdom of God is realism, not idealism. People and nations may acknowledge God's sovereign power and grace or refuse to acknowledge them. Nevertheless, God reigns over all.

This strong affirmation of God as both sovereign and engaged with the world is common to most models of the kingdom. While futurist or otherworldly models stress God's sovereignty but see little sign of God's present activity in the world, the Theocratic and Ecclesiastical Kingdom models see or seek God's present active rule in power. In contrast, the Subversive Kingdom model affirms God's power and sovereignty but stresses that God chooses to rule on earth through servanthood. The Utopian model least accents this note and in some versions flatly denies God's sovereignty or transcendence.

2. *Jesus Christ is the decisive inbreaking of the kingdom into human history.* God's reign is "the kingdom of our Lord and of his Christ" (Rev. 11:15). The good news is that in Jesus Christ, God's reign has become visible and present in love and power, though not yet fully. In Jesus' life, teachings, healings, and especially in his death and resurrection the power of the kingdom has been decisively demonstrated. "The movement of history toward its culmination in the Kingdom of God is a movement which follows the pattern of death and resurrection."[1] In the resurrection and life of Jesus we see the promise of resurrection personally and of the new heaven and new earth that will come. Jesus is Savior, Liberator, Lord, and Sovereign. He is, in the great picture of Revelation, the Lamb who is the Lion; the Lion who is the Lamb.

The nature and the character of the kingdom, therefore, always center in the person of Jesus Christ—both as the source of our spiritual life, as in the Interior and Heavenly Kingdom models, and as our model and the pattern of a new social order, as the Subversive and Transforming models show.

3. *The kingdom of God is historical.* It is not some spiritual reality that operates only in another world or that unfolds on some suprahistorical sal-

vation plane somehow parallel to our everyday existence. The kingdom is "a reality at work within history, rather than simply a goal to which history tends."[2] It is God's working down through history to fulfill his good purposes and make good on his gracious promises given in times past. Thus the kingdom moves toward the fulfillment prophesied in Scripture. The final outcome of history is sure, though we still struggle, suffer, and face doubts. We're still in the battle of the kingdom.

Here Oscar Cullmann's analogy of the significance of D-Day in World War II is particularly apt. The decisive battle has been won and victory is assured, even though the battle continues, evil appears to triumph, and many innocent people suffer.

Perhaps an even better analogy is the story of Allied prisoners in an enemy camp during World War II. Through some new prisoners who are brought to the camp, the group learns that the tide of the war has turned and Allied victory is just a matter of time. The prisoners know something their captors don't, and this gives them an extraordinary hope and resilience They still suffer; some doubt; some may die; violence may even increase as the enemy is more and more embattled. But victory will come, and the camp will be liberated.

The point is that this happens *within history*. The good news of coming victory is not just an inner hope; it is based on what is actually happening in the war. So it is with the kingdom, as given to us in Scripture. The day will come when the kingdoms of the world becomes the kingdom of God (Rev. 11:15).

The kingdom is, therefore, *teleological* in this historical sense. It moves toward the *telos,* the goal God intends. Thus Christians claim, in faith, that *history* is teleological—not random, meaningless, or merely cyclical. Some fundamental story or drama is unfolding—not blindly or by some sort of progressive evolution, but precisely as God's activity in history through those who acknowledge and serve him, and even through those who don't, as God makes the wrath of humankind praise him (Ps. 76:10).

This historical nature of the kingdom is often stressed in the last three models of our typology, and in some versions of the countersystem model. It is an essential aspect of the kingdom, but must be closely tied to Jesus' own life and work both within and beyond history.

4. *The kingdom of God promises, and is, a new social order,* a reconciled humanity and environment based on love, justice, holiness, and peace (*shalom* in the biblical sense). It promises nothing less than radical social reconstruction, "a new heaven and a new earth, the home of righteousness" (II Pet. 3:13). As we have seen, most models agree on this but disagree fundamentally as to where, when, and how this new order is to come about.

Biblically, the kingdom involves all areas of life. It is concerned with reconciliation in every sphere of human existence. God's plan is to "unite," "reconcile," or "bring together under one head" all things in Jesus Christ, as Paul repeatedly says (Eph. 1:10; Col. 1:20; II Cor. 5:19). This theme is best understood in the light of Old Testament promises of *shalom* (peace, health, harmony); of a coming age of general reconciliation, a fulfillment of the Jubilee promises.[3]

The legal code of the Sinai Covenant and, in a different way, biblical wisdom literature both point toward the new order of the kingdom. Every area of life falls within the purview of God's concern and, therefore, of holiness and wisdom. And God's plan in Christ involves the redemption of life in all its dimensions. The kingdom of God is ecological in this sense. It brings everything into view and is concerned with a proper ecological harmony throughout all of life, including matters of the spirit, the mind, the arts, the family, and all economic and political concerns. Clearly the calls for justice in Scripture must be seen in this larger context.

In this sense we may say that the kingdom is not *only* God's reign but that it is also concerned with *where* that reign is effected in space and time. Biblically the term *kingdom,* "while denoting the active rule of God, never loses its spatial dimensions as active rule calling for a place or area in which this rule finds a home," notes John Donahue.[4]

The present-day relevance of God's kingdom as suggested by this biblically holistic understanding of the kingdom has often been lost in embodiments of the Future, Interior, and Heavenly Kingdom models. It seems more likely to occur in one form or another in Theocratic, Transforming, and Utopian models, though modern-day expressions of the Subversive model also stress it.

5. *The kingdom of God is opposed by the kingdom of Satan.* A major theme in Scripture is that God's reign faces opposition. This opposition is not just human sin or sloth or self-centeredness. Nor is it merely the limitations or imperfections of earthly existence. The Bible speaks of organized, intentional opposition to God's will. Paul speaks of "the ruler of the kingdom of the air, the spirit who is now at work in those who are disobedient" (Eph. 2:2). Christians have been "rescued . . . from the dominion of darkness" and brought into God's kingdom. The classic text is Ephesians 6:12: "For our struggle is not against flesh and blood, but against the rulers, against the authorities, against the powers of this dark world and against the spiritual forces of evil in the heavenly realms." When accused of healing by demonic power, Jesus spoke of Satan's kingdom (Matt. 12:25-26 and parallels).

The kingdom of God is opposed by an array of evil powers allied with Satan; a satanic conspiracy against God's good purposes. So Christians find themselves in a battle that rages in a whole range of dimensions, from one's inner thought life to daily behavior in the world to the structures of community life to the spheres of politics, economics, and even the arts. For those with eyes to see it, there is no neutral ground. God's Spirit provides Christians with discernment to know how to live in the world so that they are working toward the kingdom of God, not its subversive alternative. This consciousness of satanic opposition is often present in the Future, Interior, and Heavenly models. It frequently is less accented or disappears from other models or is reduced to merely sociological categories.

6. *The church is not the kingdom, but is called to be the kingdom community.* The church faithfully maintains the polarity between church and kingdom by living out the reality of God's reign now, in its weakness and imperfection but in certain hope of ultimate triumph. In so doing it avoids the twin dangers of triumphalism, acting as if the kingdom had already come in fullness, and ghettoism, turning inward and acting as if the kingdom were totally irrelevant for the present world.

The mission of the church, then, is to "raise signs of the kingdom"; to be a sort of demonstration project of what the kingdom will look like when it is fully manifest. This is a difficult calling, for it means being in but not of the world. It means being salt and light in ways that its unique flavor and glow come from Jesus Christ and yet really do penetrate society.

This theme is often accented in the Subversive Kingdom model in opposition to the Ecclesiastical Kingdom, which too closely identifies the church with the kingdom.

7. *Entrance into the kingdom requires repentance, faith, and obedience.* This was John's and Jesus' starting point in announcing the kingdom: "The kingdom of God is near. Repent and believe the good news!" (Mark 1:15; see 1:4; Matt. 3:1; 4:17). The call of the kingdom is addressed to the heart and to action—not either/or, but both. The kingdom of God concerns *allegiance,* and that issue is a line running straight through every human heart and will. Kingdom living begins in the heart but extends to every area of life. As Avery Dulles wrote: "Faith is the Christian's mode of participation in that Kingdom. Insofar as we have faith, the Kingdom takes hold of us and operates in us. This means that through faith we become instruments in the healing and reconciliation of the broken world."[5]

So no one drifts into the kingdom or inherits it biologically. Jesus insisted on this in his teachings, nowhere more poignantly than in his discussion with Nicodemus. Jesus' words, "No one can see the kingdom of God unless he is born again" (John 3:3), make it clear that the kingdom is not an unconditional blessing received automatically but requires one's personal response. In the New Testament sense, evangelism is proclaiming God's kingdom so that people may respond in faith and obedience. This is often stressed in the Interior, Heavenly, and Subversive Kingdom models, though in somewhat different ways.

8. *God's reign is a kingdom of grace more than of law.* The kingdom is God's gracious reign over all things precisely because gracious love is at the heart of God's character. Though at times in the Old Testament God's judgment may appear more prominent than his grace and forgiveness, fundamentally it is always God's grace at work. God graciously provided liberation for his people and a way to approach God through sacrifice in the Old Testament economy. The acts of God under the Old Covenant find a deeper fulfillment and a more perfect, more powerful enactment in Jesus Christ and the new age of the Spirit. Jesus' life, sacrificial death, and resurrection demonstrate both God's gracious forgiveness and God's judgment on human sin, which violates God's moral character.

From the beginning of his teaching Jesus made it clear that he came neither to enforce nor to abolish the law, but to fulfill it (Matt. 5:17-48). Love, we read, "is the fulfillment of the law" (Rom. 13:10). In Jesus we see the true meaning of the kingdom and the perfect demonstration that the kingdom is not a new legalism or a universal religious or political code, but rather a new order of grace fueled by the energy of love.

Historically the church faces the extremes of legalism (a kingdom of law) or antinomianism (a kingdom of lawlessness). The biblical picture of God's kingdom is, rather, a kingdom of love and grace that reflects the moral character of God. The kingdom has a moral base because it reflects God's character, and God is holy love. This is not a kingdom without law and judgment, but it *is* a kingdom without legalism or vindictiveness. It is, above all, the kingdom of Jesus Christ, who is "the radiance of God's glory and the exact representation of his being" (Heb. 1:3).

We have seen that the Theocratic model generally ends up sacrificing grace to law in its attempt to enforce God's reign in society. Other models—particularly the Utopian and Transforming views—may go to the opposite extreme, emphasizing grace to the exclusion of God's moral law. When this happens, such views eventually run aground on the submerged sandbar of human sinfulness. The Subversive and Heavenly Kingdom models seem best to balance grace and law.

9. *The life of the kingdom is provided for us in Jesus' example and teaching.* Jesus died and rose that we might live, but he lived on earth that we might know *how* to live. In his life and suffering Jesus gives us "an example, that [we] should follow in his steps" (I Pet. 2:21). It is the power of Jesus' life in believers and collectively in the church that provides the foundation for John's words that real Christians "must walk as Jesus did" (I John 2:6). Here is the basis for ethics in the Christian community and in the world.

The Sermon on the Mount, then, becomes "the way to the kingdom." As John Wesley put it, here Jesus "is teaching the true way to life everlasting, the royal way which leads to the kingdom."[6] The sermon in Matthew 5–7 is not a new law that we must obey in order to please God and enter the kingdom. Rather it is a way of life Christians live when they have been born anew into the kingdom and Jesus lives in them by the Holy Spirit. So Jesus—his life and teaching, coupled with his death, resurrection, and ongoing reign—is the basis for life together in the Christian community and in the world. This is really Paul's point in Philippians 2, where the great hymn about Jesus' self-emptying is held forth as a model for life together in the body of Christ (Phil. 2:1-18). The life of Jesus—all he did and taught—provides the model for life together in his kingdom and for kingdom work in the world.

Christian life and witness is a warfare, but it is a warfare based on the model of Jesus, not of secular power. "For though we live in the world, we do not wage war as the world does. The weapons we fight with are not the weapons of the world," says the Apostle Paul (II Cor. 10:3-4). Yet, they are powerful for the purposes of the kingdom. One of the greatest temptations for the church is to betray the kingdom by taking up the world's weapons of violence, coercion, manipulation, and distortion of the truth.

Jesus Christ may be the central focus in futurist or "spiritual" models of the kingdom, such as the first three, though often more as the source of regeneration and inner sanctification than as the pattern for discipleship in the world. Perhaps the Subversive model best draws out the kingdom meaning of the life and example of Jesus.

10. *The kingdom comes by the mysterious working of God's sovereign Spirit, but also by human faith and obedience.* As we have seen, the polarity between divine and human action is part of the mystery of the kingdom. The church faces the twin temptations of passivity and self-reliant activisim. Scripture, however, teaches that the triune God is the primary actor in the drama of redemption, but that he seeks and expects responsible, faithful human action enabled by the Spirit. Christians are given a life to live, a cross to bear, and a kingdom to work for, but they truly fulfill their calling only as they place their confidence in God's action and allow God's Spirit to work through them.

This, apparently, was Paul's understanding when he used the term "fellow workers" or "co-workers" (*sunergoi*). We work together with God in the coming of the kingdom (see I Cor. 3:9; II Cor. 6:1; Col. 4:11). Christians who live as God intends "look forward to the day of God and speed its coming" (II Pet. 3:12). God in Christ has given men and women the high privilege of working together in history to make the kingdom fully manifest.

Here is the key function of the church as the body of Jesus Christ. Jesus has called his disciples as a people on earth to continue the works he began. Yet, if truly done in Christ, they are not our works but God's. The church is saved by grace, not works, but we are "God's workmanship, created in Christ Jesus to do good works, which God prepared in advance for us to do" (Eph. 2:10). Christians must be clear that they do not bring or build the kingdom, but neither are they to wait passively for its full realization. Christians are kingdom workers, not kingdom builders. They live and serve in the confidence that "it is God who works in [them] to will and to act according to his good purpose" (Phil. 2:13).

If the Future and Interior Kingdom models tend to slight human action in God's purposes, the Theocratic, Utopian, and in some versions the Transforming models tend to exaggerate it. Perhaps a combination of the Subversive and Transforming models would best maintain the tension.

This summary of biblical teachings on the kingdom of God shows quite clearly what the church of Jesus Christ should look like. The church is a kingdom colony, a people of God on earth called and empowered by the Spirit to show forth the reality of the kingdom *now* in assurance that the kingdom will eventually come in its fullness and that their faithful service contributes to that final fullness of God's reign. For the Christian, the kingdom always centers in Jesus Christ. Kingdom living is a question of faith and obedience. Jesus' spirit and character show us what Christian living is and what the church is to be like.

LIFE IN THE KINGDOM COMMUNITY

Jesus asks us to make our decisions and live our lives by kingdom priorities. We are to pray continually for God's kingdom to come, for God's will to be done on earth as in heaven (Matt. 6:10). Jesus' teachings tell us both how we should pray and how we should live. We are to pray for the coming of the kingdom and live the coming of the kingdom.

God's kingdom is not like any other realm, for it is the kingdom *of God*. We know what God is like by looking at Jesus Christ. Jesus came teaching and preaching the kingdom; he lived the kingdom and died in kingdom obedience.

> Therefore God exalted him to the highest place
>   and gave him the name that is above every name,
> that at the name of Jesus every knee should bow,
>   in heaven and on earth and under the earth,
> and every tongue confess that Jesus Christ is Lord,
>   to the glory of the Father. (Phil. 2:9-11)

"He must reign," Paul tells us, "until he has put all his enemies under his feet. The last enemy to be destroyed is death" (I Cor. 15:25-26).

The kingdom of God, the active reign of God over all things, is particularly the reign of Jesus, the one "like a son of man" who has been "given authority, glory and sovereign power" so that "all peoples, nations and people of every language" will worship him (Dan. 7:13-14).

Has the Christian church displaced the kingdom? To some extent it has in the minds and actions of Jesus' followers. But this was never Jesus' intent. The biblical picture is not the church *instead of* the kingdom, but rather the church as *witness to* and embryonic demonstration of the just reign of God. Thus a clear understanding of God's kingdom is essential to a proper conception of the mission of God's people, the church.

The church needs a biblical kingdom consciousness. Sensitivity to the priority of the kingdom will mean at least five things in the church.

1. Kingdom consciousness means living and working in the certain hope of the final triumph of God's reign. Christians are those who in the face of all contrary evidence affirm that God is in control and that the victory seen in the birth, life, death, resurrection, and reign of Jesus Christ is so powerful that it will eventually swallow up all evil, hate, and injustice. This gives Christians an unworldly audacious confidence that enables them to go right on doing what others say is impossible or futile.

2. Understanding God's kingdom means that the line between "sacred" and "secular" is erased. Rather than secularization of society or the sacralization of religious concerns, God's kingdom means that all things are within the sphere of God's sovereignty and, therefore, of God's concern. No room for compartmentalized thinking here. Economics, ecology, politics, the arts, social and family life—all these are kingdom topics. So kingdom Christians bring a Jesus perspective to every area of life.

3. Kingdom awareness means that ministry is much broader than church work. Christians who understand the meaning of God's reign know they are in the kingdom business, not the church business. They see all activity as ultimately having kingdom significance, so they strive (together!) to bring all things under the Lordship of Christ. They know that a secular job may be kingdom ministry if it contributes toward kingdom realities, but are ready to shift job, career, or venue if kingdom priorities so dictate.

4. In kingdom perspective, concerns of justice and evangelistic witness are necessarily held together. An awareness of God's kingdom, biblically understood, resolves the tension between these two vital concerns. Kingdom Christians want to win people to personal faith in Jesus Christ, for the line of kingdom allegiance runs straight through every human heart. They are also committed to peace, justice, and righteousness at every level of society because the circumference of the kingdom includes "all things in

heaven and on earth" (Eph. 1:10) and the welfare of every person and everything God has made. For the kingdom is, above all, a kingdom of love. Christians concerned with justice want to see as many people as possible come to faith in Jesus Christ and fidelity to his kingdom, while Christians concerned with evangelism want to see justice realized in all areas of society so the gospel will be made visibly credible. No split here.

5. Biblically speaking, the reality of the kingdom of God means that we experience *now* the first fruits of the kingdom through the Spirit. The Holy Spirit, the very Spirit of Jesus, has been given to us as a deposit, guaranteeing what is to come—namely, the kingdom in its fullness, which includes eternal life. So the Holy Spirit is "a deposit guaranteeing our inheritance" as servants of Christ and children of the kingdom (Eph. 1:14). Through faith in Jesus, Christians already experience "the powers of the coming age" (Heb. 6:5). We are to live in the power of the Spirit now—not primarily for our own benefit, but in service to the One who came to serve others and bring justice to the earth (Isa. 42:4).

God equips the Christian community with gifts of the Spirit that it may carry out its ministry of worship and witness with supernatural results. Kingdom communities, therefore, not only affirm the ministry of all believers, but they also share a life through which gifts are encouraged, called forth, and put to good use.

Kingdom Christians, then, are the community gathered around Jesus in faith, love, and service to him and to all people. They are the "little flock" to which Jesus promised the kingdom (Luke 12:32). Their greatest joy is to live in responsible community with sisters and brothers who taste the reality of the kingdom now, who live its pains and powers, and who serve in the certainty of the final triumph of the Lamb.

CONCLUSION

Depending on which models of the kingdom most truly approximate the mystery of God's purposes in history, either the kingdom will come in its final fullness within near-range history—perhaps by the year 2000, in some views—or this discussion may continue for millennia, perhaps with totally new models emerging. In this book we have traced the range of conceptions of God's reign, whether viewed from the perspective of questions of time, visibility, agency, scope, ethical character, or final goal. We have seen the complexity of kingdom models as well as the internal coherence of specific options and root metaphors.

As discussions about the kingdom continue, or perhaps as kingdom consciousness once again recedes only to emerge again in a later era, new insights and fresh angles of looking at Scripture will probably be formulated. If no fundamentally new conceptions of the kingdom emerge, yet fresh versions, variations, and hybrids of older models will probably be called forth by historical circumstances that can only be dimly imagined at present.

In the meantime, Christians who seek God's kingdom and pray for God's will to be done on earth as in heaven will experience anew the mystery and power of God's reign as they embody the good news of Jesus Christ in communities of worship and witness.

NOTES

INTRODUCTION

1. Jerald C. Brauer, "Kingdom of God," *A Handbook of Christian Theology,* ed. Marvin Halverson (New York: Living Age Books, 1958), p. 197.

2. Howard A. Snyder with Daniel V. Runyon, *Foresight* (Nashville: Thomas Nelson, 1986).

3. Garry Wills, *Under God: Religion and American Politics* (New York: Simon & Schuster, 1990), p. 24.

4. Howard A. Snyder, *The Community of the King* (Downers Grove, Ill.: InterVarsity Press, 1977); *A Kingdom Manifesto* (Downers Grove, Ill.: InterVarsity Press, 1985). I have also dealt somewhat with the kingdom in *Liberating the Church: The Ecology of Church and Kingdom* (Downers Grove, Ill.: InterVarsity Press, 1983).

5. Theodore J. Weeden, *Mark: Traditions in Conflict* (Philadelphia: Fortress Press, 1971); compare Ralph Martin, *Mark: Evangelist and Theologian* (Grand Rapids: Zondervan, 1973).

1. THE MYSTERY OF THE KINGDOM AND THE USE OF MODELS

1. Avery Dulles, *Models of the Church* (Garden City, N.Y.: Doubleday, 1974); *Models of Revelation* (Garden City, N.Y.: Doubleday, 1983).

2. See, for example, John F. O'Grady, *Models of Jesus* (Garden City, N.Y.: Doubleday, 1981); Christian Duquoc and Casiano Floristán, eds., *Models of Holiness* (New York: Seabury Press, 1979); Raymond F. Collins, *Models of Theological Reflection* (Lanham, N.J.: University Press of America, 1984); Sallie McFague, *Models of God: Theology for an Ecological Nuclear Age* (Philadelphia: Fortress Press, 1987). McFague discusses models of God as Mother, Lover, and Friend; of the world as God's Body; and critiques monarchical understandings of God.

3. H. Richard Niebuhr, *Christ and Culture* (New York: Harper & Row, 1956).

4. Dulles, *Models of Revelation,* p. 35.

5. See Matthew 13:1-52; 20:1-16; 22:1-14; 25:1-46; and parallels.

6. See Matthew 13:11; Mark 4:11; and Luke 8:10. The Greek word *mūsterion* is usually translated as "mystery" or "secret."

7. See Snyder, *The Community of the King,* pp. 15-16.

8. On the use of models in theology, see especially William F. Austin, "Models, Mystery, and Paradox in Ian Ramsey," *Journal for the Scientific Study of Religion* 7 (1968): 41-55; Ian T. Barbour, *Myths, Models, and Paradigms* (New York: Harper & Row, 1974); Ewert Cousins, "Models and the Future of Theology," *Continuum* 7 (1969): 78-91; Frederick Ferré, "Mapping the Logic of Models in Science and Theology," *The Christian Scholar* 46 (1963): 9-39; Paul Minear, *Images of the Church in the New Testament* (Philadelphia: Westminster Press, 1960); Ian T. Ramsey, *Models and Mystery* (New York: Oxford University Press, 1964) and *Religious Language* (New York: Macmillan, 1963); the extended discussion in Sallie McFague, *Metaphorical Theology: Models of God in Religious Language* (Philadelphia: Fortress Press, 1982); and Hans Küng, *Theology for the Third Millennium: An Ecumenical View,* trans. Peter Heinegg (New York: Doubleday, 1988).

9. McFague, *Metaphorical Theology*, p. 67.

10. Dulles, *Models of Revelation*, p. 30. See, similarly, Niebuhr, *Christ and Culture*, pp. 39-44.

11. Dulles, *Models of Revelation*, p. 31.

12. Ibid., p. 26.

13. See James F. Hopewell, *Congregation: Stories and Structures* (Philadelphia: Fortress Press, 1987), pp. 67-86. Hopewell says that congregations typically may be distinguished by the polarities *canonic/gnostic* and *charismatic/empiric,* yielding four primary models. (I find the terms *authority/intuition* and *spirit/experience* more clarifying.) Perhaps there is some correlation between these congregational models and models of the kingdom.

14. See Dulles's parallel discussion regarding models of revelation in *Models of Revelation,* pp. 26-27.

15. Particularly useful in this regard are John Bright, *The Kingdom of God* (Nashville: Abingdon Press, 1953); Jacques Ellul, *The Presence of the Kingdom* (New York: Seabury Press, 1967) and *The Politics of God and the Politics of Man* (Grand Rapids: Eerdmans, 1972); Donald B. Kraybill, *The Upside-Down Kingdom* (Scottsdale, Pa.: Herald Press, 1978); and George Eldon Ladd, *The Gospel of the Kingdom* (Grand Rapids: Eerdmans, 1986) and *Jesus and the Kingdom* (Waco, Tex.: Word Books, 1964).

16. See *Your Kingdom Come: Mission Perspectives,* Report on the World Conference on Mission and Evangelism (Geneva: World Council of Churches, 1980).

17. Walbert Bühlmann, *The Church of the Future: A Model for the Year 2000* (Maryknoll, N.Y.: Orbis, 1986), p. 5. Although Bühlmann is speaking of Roman Catholicism, this now holds true for Christianity generally.

18. Niebuhr's typology has, of course, been criticized from several perspectives, particularly for setting up the categories in such a way that one type emerges as preferable to the others. My point is that the usefulness and the appeal of Niebuhr's approach were due in large measure to the comprehensiveness and the simplicity of his typology.

19. McFague, *Models of God,* p. ix. William J. Everett argues that as both model and symbol kingdom language has "collapsed" for several reasons and "is no longer a fitting symbol for a position of governance." See William J. Everett, *God's Federal Republic: Reconstructing Our Governing Symbol* (New York: Paulist Press, 1988), pp. 17-18.

20. So also with the proposal to substitute "kindom" for "kingdom." There can be feuds and violence among one's kin as surely as oppression and injustice within a kingdom. While "kindom" is useful for imaging the organic, relational aspect of the church and of all humanity, it is inadequate as a substitute for "kingdom of God."

21. See Jürgen Moltmann, *The Trinity and the Kingdom* (San Francisco: Harper & Row, 1981); M. Douglas Meeks, *God the Economist: The Doctrine of God and Political Economy* (Minneapolis: Fortress Press, 1989).

22. See J. I. Packer, *Knowing God* (Downers Grove, Ill.: InterVarsity Press, 1973).

23. Tony Campolo, *The Kingdom of God Is a Party* (Dallas, Tex.: Word Books, 1990).

2. MODEL ONE: THE KINGDOM AS FUTURE HOPE

1. John Wesley, "The General Deliverance," *The Works of John Wesley,* Vol. 2, *Sermons II,* ed. Albert Outler (Nashville: Abingdon Press, 1985), p. 446.

2. John Wesley, "The New Creation," in *The Works of John Wesley,* 2:508, 510. Though Wesley's view of the kingdom is complex, as we shall see, future hope was a basic element in it.

3. Scores of New Testament passages speak of the kingdom as a future hope, most notably I Cor. 15:24-25; II Thess. 1:5; II Tim. 2:12; 4:1; 4:18; Heb. 12:28; Rev. 11:15; 12:10; 20:1-6. We will have occasion to discuss some of these as we examine other models.

4. Compare also Gal. 5:21; Eph. 5:5; I Cor. 6:9-10; 15:50. The terms *inherit* and *inheritance* occur hundreds of times in the Old Testament, often with reference to inheriting the promised land (as, for example, in Pss. 25 and 37). The Future Kingdom model, of course, interprets this theme eschatologically.

5. *The Didache,* 9:4, 10:5, *Early Christian Fathers,* ed. Cyril Richardson (New York: Macmillan, 1970), pp. 175, 176.

6. Jaroslav Pelikan, *The Emergence of the Catholic Tradition (100–600)* (Chicago: University of Chicago Press, 1971), p. 124.

7. Ibid., pp. 124-25.

8. The biblical idea behind this seems to be Eph. 1:10, which speaks of all things being brought together under the headship of Jesus Christ.

9. Irenaeus, *Against Heresies,* 32–33, in Richardson, *Early Christian Fathers,* pp. 391-94.

10. Ibid., 36:1, p. 396.

11. Tertullian, *Prescription Against Heretics,* 13, in *The Ante-Nicene Fathers,* eds. Alexander Roberts and James Donaldson (Grand Rapids: Eerdmans, 1976), 3:249. Hereafter cited as *ANF*.

12. Tertullian, *Against Marcion,* 3:25. ANF 3:342.

13. Ibid., p. 343.

14. Ibid.

15. See Jaroslav Pelikan, *The Finality of Jesus Christ in an Age of Universal History: A Dilemma of the Third Century* (Richmond: John Knox Press, 1966), p. 17.

16. Jürgen Moltmann, *The Trinity and the Kingdom,* trans. Margaret Kohl (San Franciso: Harper & Row, 1981), p. 203.

17. Ibid., p. 206.

18. Franklin H. Littell, "Radical Pietism in American History," *Continental Pietism and Early American Christianity,* ed. F. Ernest Stoeffler (Grand Rapids: Eerdmans, 1976), p. 168.

19. Joachim, *Concordia Novi ac Veteris Testamenti,* 4:33, quoted in Bernard McGinn, "The Abbot and the Doctors: Scholastic Reactions to the Radical Eschatology of Joachim of Fiore," *Church History* 40 (1971): 33.

20. Moltmann, *The Trinity and the Kingdom,* p. 204.

21. Joachim, *Concordia Novi ac Veteris Testamenti,* 5:84. Quoted in Moltmann, *The Trinity and the Kingdom,* p. 204.

22. Moltmann, *The Trinity and the Kingdom,* p. 207.

23. McGinn, "The Abbot and the Doctors," p. 35.

24. Ibid., p. 34.

25. Ibid., emphasis added.

26. See Donald W. Dayton, *Theological Roots of Pentecostalism* (Grand Rapids: Francis Asbury Press/Zondervan, 1987).

27. Robert Mapes Anderson, *Vision of the Disinherited: The Making of American Pentecostalism* (New York: Oxford University Press, 1979), p. 43. This was not uniformly the case, however; a significant portion of the Holiness Movement in the United States remained post- or amillennialist and resistant to Pentecostalism.

28. Norman Cohn, *The Pursuit of the Millennium,* rev. ed. (New York: Oxford University Press, 1970).

29. George Eldon Ladd, *Jesus and the Kingdom: The Eschatology of Biblical Realism,* 2nd ed. (Waco, Tex.: Word Books, 1969), p. 3. See also Ladd's *Crucial Questions About the Kingdom of God* (Grand Rapids: Eerdmans, 1952); *The Gospel of the Kingdom,* (London: Paternoster Press, 1959; repr., Grand Rapids: Eerdmans, 1986); *A Theology of the New Testament* (Grand Rapids: Eerdmans, 1974); *The Presence of the Future* (Grand Rapids: Eerdmans, 1974).

30. Ladd, *The Gospel of the Kingdom,* pp. 16-17.

31. James R. Coggins and Paul G. Hiebert, eds., *Wonders and the Word* (Winnipeg, Manitoba: Kindred Press, 1989), p. 19.

32. See ibid., pp. 21-22.

33. John Wimber with Kevin Springer, *Power Evangelism* (San Francisco: Harper & Row, 1986), p. xx.

34. Ibid.

35. Ibid., p. 14.

36. Ibid., p. 92. See also C. Peter Wagner, *Church Growth and the Whole Gospel* (New York: Harper & Row, 1981).

3. MODEL TWO: THE KINGDOM AS INNER SPIRITUAL EXPERIENCE

1. Kieran Kavanaugh and Otilio Rodrigues, eds., *Teresa of Avila: The Interior Castle* (New York: Paulist Press, 1979).

2. Pelikan, *The Emergence of the Catholic Tradition (100–600)*, p. 125.

3. Quoted in Pelikan, *The Emergence of the Catholic Tradition (100–600)*, p. 48.

4. Origen, *Hom. 16 in Lc.*, quoted in Everett Ferguson, ed., *Encyclopedia of Early Christianity* (New York: Garland Publishing, 1990), p. 668.

5. Robert J. Daly, "Origen," in Ferguson, *Encyclopedia of Early Christianity*, p. 668.

6. Origen, *Commentary on Matthew*, 14:7, *ANF* 10:498.

7. Origen, *On First Principles* (1:4), trans. G. W. Butterworth (Gloucester, Mass.: Peter Smith, 1973), p. 55.

8. Ibid., p. 53.

9. Ibid.

10. Origen, *Against Celsus*, 3:28, *ANF* 4:475.

11. Robert C. Gregg, ed., *Athanasius: The Life of Anthony and the Letter to Marcellinus* (New York: Paulist Press, 1980), 65.

12. Ibid., p. 46.

13. Kavanaugh and Rodrigues, *Teresa of Avila*, pp. 35, 42.

14. Quoted in ibid., p. 20.

15. Ibid.

16. Ibid., p. 195.

17. Ibid., p. 182.

18. "Teresa of Avila," *The Oxford Dictionary of the Christian Church*, 2nd ed. (London: Oxford University Press, 1974), p. 1350.

19. Georgia Harkness, *The Dark Night of the Soul* (New York: Abingdon Press, 1945).

20. Georgia Harkness, personal letter to Mrs. Carrie Stamer, May 14, 1946.

21. Georgia Harkness, *Understanding the Kingdom of God* (Nashville: Abingdon Press, 1974), p. 142.

22. See, for example, Morton T. Kelsey, *The Other Side of Silence: A Guide to Christian Meditation* (New York: Paulist Press, 1976), and *Transcend: A Guide to the Spiritual Quest* (New York: Crossroad, 1983).

23. Quoted in Roland H. Bainton, *Here I Stand* (New York: New American Library, 1955), pp. 49-50.

24. Martin Luther, *The Freedom of a Christian*, in *Martin Luther: Three Treatises*, trans. W. A. Lambert (Philadelphia: Fortress Press, 1970), pp. 288-89.

25. L. Berkhof, *The Kingdom of God: The Development of the Idea of the Kingdom, Especially Since the Eighteenth Century* (Grand Rapids: Eerdmans, 1951), p. 24.

26. Martin Luther, *The Bondage of the Will*, quoted in Paul Althaus, *The Theology of Martin Luther*, trans. Robert C. Schultz (Philadelphia: Fortress Press, 1966), p. 163.

27. Heinrich Bornkamm, *Luther's World of Thought*, trans. Martin H. Bertram (St. Louis: Concordia Publishing House, 1965), p. 245.

28. *Works of Martin Luther* (Philadelphia, 1915–32), 2:265-66. See similarly his treatise *Secular Authority* (1523).

29. See Justo L. González, *The Story of Christianity*, vol. 2 (San Francisco: Harper & Row, 1984), pp. 36-37.

30. Niebuhr, *Christ and Culture*, p. 172.

31. Ibid., p. 173.

32. John Calvin, *Institutes of the Christian Religion* 2.15.3, trans. Henry Beveridge (Grand Rapids: Eerdmans, 1975), 1:428.

33. Ibid., 2.15.4, p. 429.

34. John Calvin, "Sermons 45 and 30 on Deut.", quoted in William J. Bouwsma, *John Calvin: A Sixteenth-Century Portrait* (New York: Oxford University Press, 1988), p. 192.

35. For the political significance of Schaeffer's critique of culture and its influence on the current abortion debate in the United States, see Garry Wills, *Under God: Religion and American Politics* (New York: Simon and Schuster, 1990), chap. 28, "Evangelicals: Francis Schaeffer," pp. 318-28.

36. Hannah Whitall Smith, *The Christian's Secret of a Happy Life* (Westwood, N.J.: Fleming H. Revell, 1952). In its original 1870 edition this was one of the first books published by Revell.

37. Carl F. H. Henry, *God, Revelation and Authority,* vol. 2 (Waco, Tex.: Word Books, 1976), p. 30.

38. Ibid., p. 36.

39. Ibid.

40. Carl F. H. Henry, *God, Revelation and Authority,* vol. 6 (Waco, Tex.: Word Books, 1983), p. 420.

41. Carl F. H. Henry, *A Plea for Evangelical Demonstration* (Grand Rapids: Baker Book House, 1971), pp. 66, 117.

42. Charles Colson with Ellen Santilli Vaughn, *Kingdoms in Conflict* (New York: William Morrow and Zondervan Publishing House, 1987), p. 86.

43. Ibid., pp. 87, 94. Colson particularly affirms the perspective of the church's social role articulated in Richard John Neuhaus, *The Naked Public Square* (Grand Rapids: Eerdmans, 1986).

44. For example, in Julian of Norwich. See Edmund Colledge and James Walsh, eds., *Julian of Norwich: Showings* (New York: Paulist Press, 1978), pp. 8-11.

45. For example, Rosemary Radford Ruether and Sallie McFague. (This would generally be true as well for other varieties of liberation theology.)

46. Luther and Calvin are certainly no exception here. Our secularized age tends to be impressed with Luther's mundane, this-worldly, sometimes irreverent comments and tends to forget that this former Augustinian monk lived in an age when faith was often too otherworldly and needed fleshing out in everyday life. This, however, was simply the practical earthly application of the meaning of the interior reality of salvation by faith in Christ—not a transmutation of the kingdom of God into mere politics, economics, or social ethics.

47. Similarly, much of the earthiness of Old Testament wisdom literature is spiritualized in this model. The Song of Solomon, for example, is viewed as a picture of the love of Christ for the church or the soul.

4. MODEL THREE: THE KINGDOM AS MYSTICAL COMMUNION

1. Wilhelm Breuning, "Communion of Saints," *Encyclopedia of Theology: The Concise Sacramentum Mundi,* ed. Karl Rahner (New York: Seabury Press, 1975), p. 274.

2. See Dietrich Bonhoeffer, *The Communion of Saints,* trans. R. Gregor Smith (New York: Harper & Row, 1960). Bonhoeffer describes the church (the "communion of saints") as the kingdom of Christ, which in faith and hope awaits the full coming of the kingdom of God.

3. Dulles, *Models of the Church,* p. 107.

4. Ibid.

5. See Jaroslav Pelikan, *The Spirit of Eastern Christendom (600–1700)* (Chicago: University of Chicago Press, 1974), pp. 261, 266; Colm Luibheid and Norman Russell, trans., *John Climacus: The Ladder of Divine Ascent* (New York: Paulist Press, 1982), pp. 1-2, 56.

6. Richard Baxter, *The Saints' Everlasting Rest* (New York: American Tract Society, n.d.), p. 442.

7. John Wesley, "The Way to the Kingdom," *Works* 1:220.

8. John Wesley, sermon, "The Reformation of Manners," *Works,* 2:302.

9. John Wesley, sermon, "Upon our Lord's Sermon on the Mount," First Discourse, *Works,* 1:470.

10. Ibid., p. 481.

11. John Wesley, "Upon Our Lord's Sermon on the Mount," Second Discourse, *Works,* 1:509.

12. Thomas C. Oden, *The Word of Life,* Systematic Theology, vol. 2 (San Francisco: Harper & Row, 1989), p. 521.

13. Ibid., pp. 523-24.

14. Ibid., pp. 522-23.

15. Ibid., pp. 516, 517.
16. Colleen McDannell and Bernhard Lang, *Heaven: A History* (New Haven: Yale University Press, 1988), p. 98.
17. Quoted in ibid., p. 101. In this connection one might consider also the sensual and sometimes erotic imagery found among the Moravians under Count Zinzendorf in the mid-1700s.
18. See Evelyn Underhill, *Mysticism: A Study in the Nature and Development of Man's Spiritual Consciousness,* 12th ed. (New York: Meridian Books, 1956), pp. 393, 420-21.
19. Revivalist Christianity, which also exemplifies this model, may place less emphasis on the Eucharist but may functionally embue other things with sacramental power—the testimony meeting, the love feast, or the altar call, for example.

5. MODEL FOUR: THE KINGDOM AS INSTITUTIONAL CHURCH

1. I use the term *ecclesiastical* rather than *ecclesial* to suggest not simply an identification of the kingdom with the church but specifically with the church in its organized institutional form.
2. Augustine, *The City of God,* trans. Marcus Dods (New York: The Modern Library, 1950), pp. 725-26.
3. Archibald Robertson, *Regnum Dei: Eight Lectures on the Kingdom of God in the History of Christian Thought* (New York: Macmillan, 1901), p. 193.
4. Pelikan, *The Emergence of the Catholic Tradition (100–600),* p. 129.
5. Peter L. Berger, *The Noise of Solemn Assemblies: Christian Commitment and the Religious Establishment in America* (Garden City, N.Y.: Doubleday, 1961), pp. 59-60.
6. Ibid., p. 63.
7. It is useful to compare Berger's perspective with that of Garry Wills in his recent book *Under God: Religion and American Politics.* Wills suggests that American politics cannot be accurately understood without reference to the role of religion in the social and political life of the United States.
8. Stanley Hauerwas and William H. Willimon, *Resident Aliens: Life in the Christian Colony* (Nashville: Abingdon Press, 1989). The book title immediately signals a shift in models.
9. C. Peter Wagner, *Church Growth and the Whole Gospel: A Biblical Mandate* (San Francisco: Harper & Row, 1981), p. 9.
10. Ibid., p. 10.
11. Ibid., p. 11. See J. G. Davies, "Church Growth: A Critique," *International Review of Missions* 57:267 (July 1968): 293.
12. Mortimer Arias, *Announcing the Reign of God: Evangelization and the Subversive Memory of Jesus* (Philadelphia: Fortress Press, 1984), p. 118.
13. Orlando E. Costas, *Christ Outside the Gate: Mission Beyond Christendom* (Maryknoll, N.Y.: Orbis Books, 1982), pp. 43-44.
14. See Dulles, *Models of the Church*; Snyder, *Liberating the Church,* chap. 4.

6. MODEL FIVE: THE KINGDOM AS COUNTERSYSTEM

1. Literally, "has been pleased to give you . . . ," but "delights" (my translation) better brings out the intended sense.
2. See Howard A. Snyder, *A Kingdom Manifesto* (Downers Grove, Ill.: InterVarsity Press, 1985).
3. See Franklin H. Littell, "The Concept of the Believers' Church," James Leo Garrett, Jr., *The Concept of the Believers' Church* (Scottsdale, Pa.: Herald Press, 1969), p. 27; John Howard Yoder, *The Priestly Kingdom: Social Ethics as Gospel* (Notre Dame: University of Notre Dame Press, 1984), pp. 124-25.
4. Yoder, *The Priestly Kingdom,* p. 92.

5. G. K. Chesterton, *St. Francis of Assisi* (Garden City, N.Y.: Image Books, 1957), p. 16.

6. Regis J. Armstrong and Ignatius C. Brady, trans., *Francis and Clare: The Complete Works* (New York: Paulist Press, 1982), p. 105.

7. Ibid., p. 111.

8. Ibid., p. 122.

9. Ibid., p. 141.

10. Ibid., pp. xv, 13.

11. Ibid., p. 16.

12. See Albrecht Ritschl, "Prolegomena" *The History of Pietism*, in Ritschl, *Three Essays*, trans. Philip Hefner (Philadelphia: Fortress Press, 1972), pp. 53-147.

13. See especially John Howard Yoder, *The Politics of Jesus* (Grand Rapids: Eerdmans, 1972) and Donald F. Durnbaugh, *The Believers' Church: The History and Character of Radical Protestantism* (New York: Macmillan, 1968).

14. Ronald J. Sider, *Rich Christians in an Age of Hunger* (Downers Grove, Ill.: InterVarsity Press, 1977); Donald B. Kraybill, *The Upside-Down Kingdom* (Scottsdale, Pa.: Herald Press, 1978); André Trocmé, *Jesus and the Nonviolent Revolution* (Scottsdale, Pa.: Herald Press, 1973); Mortimer Arias, *Announcing the Reign of God: Evangelization and the Subversive Memory of Jesus* (Philadelphia: Fortress Press, 1984); Andrew Kirk, *The Good News of the Kingdom Coming* (Downers Grove, Ill.: InterVarsity Press, 1983).

15. Hauerwas and Willimon, *Resident Aliens: Life in the Christian Colony*, pp. 87, 88-89, 90.

16. I have explored this issue more fully in *Signs of the Spirit,* particularly pp. 270-81, 290-91, 302-3. More thoughtful and knowledgeable proponents of this model, such as John Howard Yoder, are of course aware of this issue and have developed perspectives concerning Christian witness within and to structures.

17. An excellent presentation of this perspective on the book of Revelation is Ted Grimsrud, *Triumph of the Lamb* (Scottsdale, Pa.: Herald Press, 1987).

18. See Snyder, *Signs of the Spirit*, pp. 52-61.

7. MODEL SIX: THE KINGDOM AS POLITICAL STATE

1. Jaroslav Pelikan, *The Excellent Empire: The Fall of Rome and the Triumph of the Church* (San Francisco: Harper & Row, 1987), p. 75.

2. Ibid., pp. 77-78.

3. Jerald C. Brauer, ed., *The Westminster Dictionary of Church History* (Philadelphia: Westminster Press, 1971), p. 814.

4. Roland H. Bainton, *The Reformation of the Sixteenth Century,* enlarged ed. (Boston: Beacon Press, 1985), pp. 117-18.

5. John T. McNeill, *The History and Character of Calvinism* (London: Oxford University Press, 1973), p. 185.

6. Georgia Harkness, *John Calvin: The Man and His Ethics* (New York: Abingdon, 1931), p. 22.

7. John Calvin, Sermon on 1 Samuel 42. Quoted in W. Fred Graham, *The Constructive Revolutionary: John Calvin and His Socio-Economic Impact* (Richmond: John Knox Press, 1971), pp. 158-59.

8. Graham, *The Constructive Revolutionary,* p. 158.

9. Ibid., p. 176. See also Bouwsma, *John Calvin,* pp. 208-13.

10. Commentary on Psalm 82:3, quoted in Graham, *The Constructive Revolutionary,* p. 62.

11. Niebuhr, *Christ and Culture,* pp. 217-18.

12. Wilhelm Pauck, ed., *Melanchthon and Bucer, The Library of Christian Classics* (Philadelphia: Westminster Press, 1969), p. 157.

13. See ibid., p. 171.

14. Martin Bucer, *De Regno Christi,* in ibid., pp. 175-76.

15. Ibid., p. 178.

16. Ibid., p. 185.

17. Ibid., p. 227.

18. Ibid., p. 225.

19. Ibid., p. 211.

20. Ibid., p. 209.

21. Ibid., pp. 208-9. How people view Constantine and the subsequent political recognition of Christianity, whether positively (Bucer, Jonathan Edwards) or negatively (Anabaptists, John Wesley), is a key indicator of their models of church and kingdom.

22. Ibid., p. 386.

23. See ibid., pp. 172-73.

24. See Leo F. Solt, "The Fifth Monarchy Men: Politics and the Millennium," *Church History* 30 (1961): 314-24.

25. H. Richard Niebuhr, *The Kingdom of God in America* (New York: Harper and Bros., 1959), p. 45.

26. Sherwood Eddy, *The Kingdom of God and the American Dream* (New York: Harper and Bros., 1941), p. 30.

27. Arthur M. Schlesinger, Jr., *The Cycles of American History* (Boston: Houghton Mifflin Company, 1986), p. 19.

28. Ibid., pp. 14, 15.

29. Ibid., p. 14.

30. See Walter Nicgorski and Ronald Weber, eds., *An Almost Chosen People: The Moral Aspirations of Americans* (Notre Dame: University of Notre Dame Press, 1976).

31. The best source on Hong Xiuquan (old style: Hung Hsiu-ch'üan) and his movement is Jen Yu-wen, *The Taiping Revolutionary Movement* (New Haven: Yale University Press, 1973), though there are many other sources, including *The Taiping Revolution,* authored by the Compilation Group for the "History of Modern China" Series (Peking: Foreign Languages Press, 1976).

32. Hugh Deane, *Good Deeds and Gunboats: Two Centuries of American-Chinese Encounters* (San Francisco: China Books and Periodicals, 1990), p. 216.

33. Jen Yu-wen, *The Taiping Revolutionary Movement,* p. 28.

34. Ibid., p. 155.

35. "Hung Hsiu-Chu'üan's Annotations to the New Testament," in Franz Michael, *The Taiping Rebellion: History and Documents,* vol. 2 (Seattle: University of Seattle Press, 1971), p. 227.

36. Ibid., pp. 231, 235.

37. Jen Yu-wen, *The Taiping Revolutionary Movement,* pp. 7-8. An estimated twenty to fifty million Chinese died in the revolution and its suppression. Ho Ping-ti wrote, "The Taiping Rebellion is deservedly called the greatest civil war in world history. In sheer brutality and destruction it has few peers in the annals of history" (*Studies on the Population of China* [Cambridge, Mass.: Harvard University Press, 1959], p. 247).

38. Quoted in *The Taiping Revolution* (1976), p. 41.

39. John King Fairbank, *The Great Chinese Revolution: 1800-1985* (New York: Harper & Row, 1987), pp. 75-76.

40. W. A. P. Martin, *A Cycle of Cathay* (New York: Fleming H. Revell, 1897), p. 142.

41. Kenneth Scott Latourette, *A History of Christian Missions in China* (New York: Macmillan, 1929), pp. 301-2.

42. Pat Robertson with Bob Slosser, *The Secret Kingdom* (Nashville: Thomas Nelson, 1982), pp. 36, 37.

43. See ibid., pp. 151-53.

44. William S. Barker and W. Robert Godfrey, eds., *Theonomy: A Reformed Critique* (Grand Rapids: Zondervan, 1990), p. 9.

45. David Chilton, *Paradise Restored: An Eschatology of Dominion* (Tyler, Tex.: Reconstruction Press, 1988), p. 5. See Rousas John Rushdoony, *The Institutes of Biblical Law* (Phillipsburg, N.J.: Presbyterian and Reformed Publishing Co., 1973).

46. Greg Bahnsen, *Theonomy in Christian Ethics,* quoted in Hal Lindsey, *The Road to Holocaust* (New York: Bantam Books, 1989), p. 33.

47. Barker and Godfrey, *Theonomy,* p. 10.

48. Ibid., pp. 9-10.

49. Garry Wills comments on this link between Dominion Theology and Robertson's views in *Under God: Religion and American Politics,* p. 174.

8. MODEL SEVEN: THE KINGDOM AS CHRISTIANIZED CULTURE

1. See Johann Albrecht Bengel, *Gnomon Novi Testamenti,* 3rd ed. (London: Williams & Norgate, 1862), pp. 1059-60.

2. See Donald W. Dayton, *Discovering an Evangelical Heritage* (New York: Harper & Row, 1976).

3. Donald K. Gorrell, *The Age of Social Responsibility: The Social Gospel in the Progressive Era, 1900–1920* (Macon: Mercer University Press, 1988), pp. 127-29.

4. Ibid., pp. 129-30.

5. Walter Rauschenbusch, *A Theology for the Social Gospel* (New York: Macmillan, 1917), p. 142.

6. Walter Rauschenbusch, *Christianity and the Social Crisis* (New York: Macmillan, 1907), p. 71. By March 1911, this book had already been reprinted ten times.

7. Ibid., p. 351.

8. Rauschenbusch, *A Theology for the Social Gospel,* pp. 134-37.

9. Walter Rauschenbusch, "The Kingdom of God," *Cleveland Young Men* 27 (January 9, 1913): unpaginated.

10. Rauschenbusch, *Christianity and the Social Crisis,* p. 345.

11. William Booth, "Salvation for Both Worlds," *All the World* 5:1 (January 1889): 1-2.

12. E. Stanley Jones, *A Song of Ascents: A Spiritual Autobiography* (Nashville: Abingdon Press, 1968), pp. 148-49.

13. E. Stanley Jones, *Christ's Alternative to Communism* (Nashville: Abingdon Press, 1935), pp. 41-42. The book was reprinted twice during its first year.

14. Ibid., p. 55.

15. Ibid., p. 48.

16. Ibid., p. 31.

17. David Bundy, "The Theology of the Kingdom of God in E. Stanley Jones," *Wesleyan Theological Journal* 23:1/2 (Spring-Fall 1988): 68.

18. E. Stanley Jones, *The Unshakable Kingdom and the Unchanging Person* (Nashville: Abingdon Press, 1972), p. 65. See Jones, *Is the Kingdom of God Realism?* (Nashville: Abingdon Press, 1940).

19. E. Stanley Jones, *Victorious Living* (New York: Abingdon Press, 1936), p. 316.

20. Bundy, "The Theology of the Kingdom of God in E. Stanley Jones," p. 73.

9. MODEL EIGHT: THE KINGDOM AS EARTHLY UTOPIA

1. Quoted in Lewis Mumford, *The Story of Utopias* (New York: Viking Press, 1962), title page.

2. Ibid., p. 2.

3. *The Merriam-Webster Pocket Dictionary* (New York: Pocket Books, 1958), p. 407.

4. Mumford, *The Story of Utopias,* p. 111.

5. Mark Holloway, *Heavens on Earth: Utopian Communities in America 1680–1880,* 2nd ed. (New York: Dover Publications, 1966), p. 18. See also Rosemary Radford Ruether, *The Radical Kingdom: The Western Experience of Messianic Hope* (New York: Paulist Press, 1970), chap. 4.

6. John L. Thomas, "Antislavery and Utopia," in Martin Duberman, ed., *The Antislavery Vanguard: New Essays on the Abolitionists* (Princeton, N.J.: Princeton University Press, 1965), p. 256.

7. Quoted in Holloway, *Heavens on Earth,* p. 125.

8. Ibid., p. 210.

9. See Norman Cohn, *The Pursuit of the Millennium,* rev. ed. (New York: Oxford, 1970).

10. Avery Dulles, "The Meaning of Faith Considered in Relationship to Justice," in John C. Haughey, ed., *The Faith That Does Justice: Examining the Christian Sources for Social Change* (New York: Paulist Press, 1977), p. 35.

11. Gustavo Gutiérrez, *A Theology of Liberation: History, Politics and Salvation,* trans. Caridad Inda and John Eagleson (Maryknoll, N.Y.: Orbis Books, 1973), p. 177.

12. There is, of course, a broad range of feminist theologies, as there is of liberation theologies. Those who call themselves "biblical feminists" (whose theology is avowedly Evangelical) would better fit the countersystem model, perhaps in combination with earlier models. As hinted in chapter 3, the accent on experience, and on the affective dimension generally, constitutes an element of affinity between the Utopian and Interior Kingdom models. Womanist theology, which insists on the need to deal with the twin oppressions of race and sex in the experience of black women, is a distinct variant of feminist theology and probably best embodies the Subversive, Interior, and Heavenly models, combining elements of all three (partly because of the influence of the African American Christian tradition). Thus womanist theology may find itself closer to biblical feminism than to radical feminist theology.

13. Sallie McFague, "An Earthly Theological Agenda," *The Christian Century* 108:1 (January 2-9, 1991): 12-15.

14. Ibid., p. 12.

15. Teilhard de Chardin, *The Future of Man* (New York: Harper Torchbooks, 1969), p. 74.

16. A similar perspective in terms of the conception of God's kingdom is found in Tissa Balasuriya, *Planetary Theology* (Maryknoll, N.Y.: Orbis Books, 1984). Balasuriya argues that "a shift of accent from a church-centered theology to a kingdom-centered theology will inspire Christians to be more concerned with their neighbor and human society than with their own personal interests" (p. 169). However, Balasuriya's "cosmic Christ" is more "the principle of a universal human solidarity" than the historic Jesus; we must discover "the magnificent vision of the understanding of all reality as in Christ or 'christic' " (p. 187); and his understanding of the kingdom seems more evolutionary than either historical or transcendent.

10. KINGDOM MODELS AND CHRISTIAN FAITHFULNESS

1. E. Stanley Jones, *Is the Kingdom of God Realism?* (New York: Abingdon Press, 1940), pp. 58-59.

2. Ibid., pp. 59-60.

3. Garry Wills makes this point with regard to the political impact of millenarian thinking in the United States in *Under God: Religion and American Politics.* See especially pp. 127-43.

4. While most modern biblical translations do not use the term *dispensation,* it is found four times in the King James Version of the New Testament, in each case translating the Greek term *oikonomia* ("economy" or "stewardship"). Ephesians 1:10, for example, has "the dispensation of the fulness of time" in the KJV; "plan for the fulness of time" in the RSV; and "to be put into effect when the times will have reached their fulfillment" in the NIV. Timothy Weber notes that the term *dispensation* "originates from *oikonomeo* and its derivatives, which appear about twenty times in the Greek New Testament and mean 'to manage, regulate, administer, and plan the affairs of a household.'... When used of God, the word refers to his sovereign plan for the world." T. P. Weber, "Dispensationalism," in Daniel G. Reid, ed., *Dictionary of Christianity in America* (Downers Grove, Ill.: InterVarsity Press, 1990), p. 358.

5. Clarence B. Bass, *Backgrounds to Dispensationalism* (Grand Rapids: Eerdmans, 1960), p. 19. Bass's critique of dispensationalism generally has the modern premillennial form in view. He says, "The distinguishing features of dispensationalism do not involve merely a chronology of events about the end times, as important as this may be, but involve some basic principles of interpretation that depart radically from the historic Christian faith, and that are often diametrically opposed to what the church always believed" (p. 17). This comment certainly applies to modern premillennial dispensationalism; however, in general dispensational theories may be more or less compatible with historic Christian orthodoxy, depending on their hermeneutical basis.

6. Lewis Sperry Chafer, *Major Bible Themes* (Chicago: Moody Press, 1944), p. 96. Scofield (1843–1921) constructed the highly influential *Scofield Reference Bible* (1909), which popularized the dispensational premillennialism of John Nelson Darby (1800–1882), British Plymouth Brethren leader. According to Scofield, a dispensation is "a period of time during which man is tested in respect to some specific revelation of the will of God." "These periods are marked off in Scripture by some change in God's method of dealing with mankind, in respect to two questions: of sin, and of man's responsibility. Each of the dispensations may be regarded as a new test of the natural man, and each ends in judgment—marking his utter failure in every dispensation" (*Scofield Reference Bible*).

7. Solt, "The Fifth Monarchy Men," p. 315.

8. For this reason, dispensationalism was given only passing mention in the presentation of the eight models in the preceding chapters.

9. Jonathan Edwards, *A History of the Work of Redemption Containing the Outlines of a Body of Divnity in a Method Entirely New* (Edinburgh, 1774; Philadelphia: Presbyterian Board of Education, n.d.), pp. 219-20. See also Howard Snyder, *Signs of the Spirit*, pp. 42-45.

10. See George E. Ladd, *The Blessed Hope* (Grand Rapids: Eerdmans, 1956), p. 28.

11. Bass, *Backgrounds to Dispensationalism*, p. 16.

12. Loraine Boettner, *The Millennium* (Philadelphia: Presbyterian and Reformed Publishing Co., 1964), p. 150.

13. Obviously this would not be true for someone who sees God as totally immanent and not at all ontologically, personally transcendent beyond human consciousness or existence.

14. In a sense, the strength of models as a theological method is also its weakness. Models show that an issue or phenomenon can be viewed from different angles and understood in differing ways. This is helpful for clarity, but can also lead to total relativism. Is there any way to mediate between models in the search for truth? Are there any controls or restraints on the relativism that the use of models seems to imply?

Simply at the human level, there are certain constraints inherent in the fact that models are always used within some particular social context, some community of discourse. Within the scientific community, for instance, cumulative tradition and understandings provide the context for meaning as different models are explored. This, then, provides the basis for testing the validity and usefulness of new models within the community, both in terms of how they "feel" and "fit" within the community and as tested by further study and experimentation.

Something more is at stake, however, within the Christian community. Here it is a question, in part, of "faith seeking understanding." Christian theological reflection (as distinct from other varieties) properly starts from the conviction that God has acted decisively in Jesus Christ to bring people into reconciled fellowship with God and with one another and ultimately to heal the world. By faith, Christians confess that this is the central truth transcending all our models and toward which, in various ways, all our models point. Biblically speaking, this is by definition what distinguishes a Christian from a non-Christian model of reality and of truth. It is, therefore, the Megamodel, the fundamental framework by which everything else is to be tested.

This does not totally remove "subjectivity" or relativism, of course, for it is human beings and communities that interpret who Jesus Christ is and what he means for us and for the world. Yet, Jesus Christ, as attested in Scripture and then in Christian tradition and experience, does provide the fundamental paradigm by which everything else is to be tested. And our subjectivity is limited significantly by the Scriptures and by our life together within the Christian community.

I would therefore argue for what might be called a "metapluralist" approach to hermeneutics: a stance that views all that is, in all its multiplurality, as standing vis-à-vis the Creator God with whom, ultimately, all of us will have to do.

For the interpreter, this is a stance of third naivete (to adapt Ricoeurian terms) in which the focus has shifted conceptually from the receptive and reflective knower to the One who knows and makes known. This is a stance beyond (or above) a precritical first naivete, a critical hermeneutic of suspicion, and a postcritical second naivete, which from a metapluralist perspective is still naive because it is human-centered. The approach I am suggesting cycles through hermeneutical suspicion about postcriticality to another level of naivete. If it be argued that this is impossible because one cannot step so totally outside oneself, the answer is twofold: (1) our minds do in fact give us the capacity to step conceptually outside ourselves; and (2) something in the human mind or spirit is attuned to receiving God's revelation when we are willing thus to open ourselves to truth that is beyond or above us.

A metapluralist stance of third naivete admits that this is a position of *faith*. It admits to being childlike. It also insists, however, that this is no more a stance of faith than are the other options, for ultimately in these matters one is forced back to the question of what one *believes* about the nature of reality and of the structure of meaning.

The personal question then becomes: Which model best fits or consists with one's own experience (in all its dimensions—emotional, volitional, and rational, including both logical and analogical), with shared human experience (past and present), and with the world of information and data available to us?

This model is radically theist, as is Scripture. All other models are radically humanist, as is most intellectual theorizing today.

Since this is a faith stance, not a scientific (i.e., inductive) or logical (i.e., deductive) one, it is a position of both confidence and humility—the confidence born of faith and the humility born of grace. From this perspective, the question is not so much how I may know meaning or truth, but how I may come to know that I am known and loved of God.

15. Dulles, *Models of the Church,* pp. 180-83.

16. Niebuhr, *Christ and Culture,* pp. 238-39.

17. Howard A. Snyder, *A Kingdom Manifesto* (Downers Grove, Ill.: InterVarsity Press, 1985), pp. 74-75.

18. Dulles, *Models of the Church,* p. 30.

11. THE GOSPEL OF THE KINGDOM AND THE GLOBAL ECONOMY

1. Norman J. Ornstein and Mark Schmitt, "Dateline Campaign '92: Post-Cold War Politics," *Foreign Policy* 79 (Summer 1990): 169-86.

2. See M. Douglas Meeks, *God the Economist: the Doctrine of God and Political Economy* (Minneapolis: Fortress Press, 1989).

3. Statistics primarily from David B. Barrett, ed., *World Christian Encyclopedia* (Nairobi: Oxford University Press, 1982).

4. Bühlmann, *The Church of the Future: A Model for the Year 2000,* pp. 4-6.

5. I argued essentially these same points in *Liberating the Church: The Ecology of Church and Kingdom* (Downers Grove, Ill.: InterVarsity Press, 1983), pp. 37-67.

6. Walter Brueggemann, *The Land* (Philadelphia: Fortress Press, 1977), pp. 2-3.

7. See Kenneth P. Alpers, "Starting Points for an Ecological Theology: A Bibliographic Survey," in Martin E. Marty and Dean G. Peerman, eds., *New Theology No. 8* (New York: Macmillan, 1971), p. 305.

8. C. S. Lewis, "Myth Became Fact," *God in the Dock* (Grand Rapids: Eerdmans, 1970), 66-67.

9. There is, of course, a large genre of Christian fantasy literature that seeks to make believable the reality of the spiritual dimension and the interface between the two. Recently Frank Peretti's best-selling split-level novels, *This Present Darkness* and *Piercing the Darkness,* offer a somewhat simplistic, less nuanced attempt to do what Lewis did more profoundly.

10. There is space here only to suggest, not fully elaborate, this model. Its elaboration would require dealing with the category of history as well as with myth and story. Herbert Butterfield hinted at the usefulness of the dramatic model in *Christianity and History,* suggesting the analogy of a composer and an orchestral composition in envisaging God's activity. What he says about history might equally be applied to the kingdom of God: "It is better worldly-wisdom, even when we are only looking for a pictorial representation, to think of history as though an intelligence were moving over the story, taking its bearings afresh after everything men do, and making its decisions as it goes along. . . . There is no symbolic representation that will do justice to history save [that of] the composer . . . who composes the music as we go along, and, when we slip into aberrations, switches his course in order to make the best of

everything." Herbert Butterfield, *Christianity and History* [1949] (London: Fontana Books, 1964), p. 143.

12. BUILDING KINGDOM COMMUNITIES TODAY

1. David Hollenbach, "Modern Catholic Teachings Concerning Justice," in John C. Haughey, ed., *The Faith That Does Justice: Examining the Christian Sources for Social Change* (New York: Paulist Press, 1977), p. 227.

2. Avery Dulles, "The Meaning of Faith Considered in Relationship to Justice," in Haughey, *The Faith That Does Justice,* p. 13.

3. See Howard A. Snyder, *A Kingdom Manifesto,* chaps. 1–7.

4. John R. Donahue, "Biblical Perspectives on Justice," in Haughey, *The Faith That Does Justice,* p. 86.

5. Dulles, "The Meaning of Faith Considered in Relationship to Justice," p. 43.

6. John Wesley, "Upon Our Lord's Sermon on the Mount," Discourse the First, *The Works of John Wesley,* vol. 1 (Nashville: Abingdon Press, 1984), p. 470.

INDEX